"In today's fractured world, theology
trasts existing among the great relig
lifetime exploring Scripture, enlight
of the significance of the hymn in P
light on the mystery of Jesus. Lounib
Christian humility and the Buddhist tradition of nothingness, laying common ground for mutual understanding while recognizing real differences."

—L. PATRICK CARROLL
author of *A Crooked Finger Beckons*

"John Lounibos has written a scholarly work of the first order. His extensive research into the topic of 'kenosis' has resulted in a work of profound importance. It deserves to be studied by those involved in biblical study and in the related work of renewing communities of faith, as well as by those who focus on spiritual and philosophical renewal, either within the Eastern or the Western traditions, including those engaged by various disciplines sometimes grouped under the heading of depth psychology."

—WILLIAM J. HURST
Faculty member at the Center for Modern Psychoanalytic Studies

"Christian dialogue with Buddhism is today both interesting and necessary. In this clear, compelling, and most opportune study, theologian John Lounibos explores how the stirring Pauline hymn in Philippians 2 on the 'self-emptying' of Christ Jesus, a theme developed in the 'kenotic spirituality' of Paul Tillich, mirrors the 'non-self' teaching of Buddhism, and provides us an invaluable contact point for mutual dialogue and understanding."

—G. DONALD MALONEY
Collegiate Professor, Psychology and Philosophy, University of Maryland

"This collection represents over forty years of research, inter-religious dialogue, and personal spiritual practice. Lounibos asks us to consider what the self-emptying of Christ implies for inter-religious dialogue, as well as our own inner spiritual life. The essay on Paul Tillich is inspired by his genius in converting biblical symbols into existential language that strikes at the heart of our human, anxious, experiences. Christ is the New Being, who overcomes estrangement and empowers our weakened, finite freedom. Dialogue with Zen Buddhist scholar Masao Abe compares the Philippians hymn with the teaching of *śūnyatā* or 'nothingness'(no mental concept or self-focused desire) in the 'Heart Sutra.'"

—MICHAEL R. SASO
Professor of Buddhist, Daoist, Spirituality Studies, Beijing and Los Angeles

Self-Emptying of Christ and the Christian

Self-Emptying of Christ and the Christian

Three Essays on Kenosis

John B. Lounibos

WIPF & STOCK · Eugene, Oregon

SELF-EMPTYING OF CHRIST AND THE CHRISTIAN
Three Essays on Kenosis

Wipf & Stock
An Imprint of Wipf and Stock Publishers
199 W. 8th Ave., Suite 3
Eugene, OR 97401

www.wipfandstock.com

ISBN 13: 978-1-61097-189-8

Manufactured in the U.S.A.

To

John (1903–2002) & Elrose (1903–90)
Anne Marie, Mark & Mandy, Kristin & Jason
Sophia, Lucy, Elena, Henry, Daniel
Bill (1927–88), Renee, Guy, Paul, Philip, Anne
and all my Teachers and Students.

Contents

Acknowledgments

Many thanks to Amy Haase-Thomas, assistant librarian at the Sullivan Library of Dominican College, Blauvelt, New York, for diligently finding books to assist some updates for this work. Thanks to Katie Brittany, assistant director of graduate admissions at Dominican College, for retyping the first essay onto a computer to enable me to edit the text. Special thanks go to Robert R. Rahl, who copy-edited the text, reformatted the notes, and offered many suggestions for improvement.

For careful, critical, and encouraging reading of the entire work by Edward L. Burke, L. Patrick Carroll, Roger J. Guettinger, William J. Hurst, G. Donald Maloney, Michael J. McDermott Jr., Michael R. Saso, and George B. York II, heart-felt thanks to all.

Prologue

THE THREE essays assembled here were written over a forty-year period. "Self-emptying" refers to the Greek phrase *heauton ekenōsen*. The hymn to Christ in St. Paul's letter to the Philippians uses this expression and is the inspiration for this writing. The hymn says that Christ "emptied himself" (Phil 2:7). *Kenosis* is a shorthand word to summarize this self-emptying. The example of Christ is presented by Paul as a model for Christian virtue in the community of early Christians who received the letter.

This prologue provides a narrative that briefly maps those forty years of intellectual and spiritual journeying with the Philippians letter in mind. It explains the setting for my interest in the hymn to Christ. It signals three crossroads, occasioned by historical circumstances, that moved kenosis research from biblical study, through one phase of historical development, to current interfaith conversations between Christianity and Buddhism. The last two essays also touch briefly on features of the Russian Orthodox mystical kenoticism, a popular form of Christian piety filled with tones of self-surrender, that offered no religious resistance to dictatorial governments.

Each essay represents a different task in the craft of theology. The first is a study of the language of the hymn to Christ in Paul's letter to the Philippians. Completed in 1967, it engages several techniques of exegesis in service of theology. The second essay analyzes historical antecedents to discern remnants of the emptying theme in the theology of Paul Tillich (1886–1965), a German-American Lutheran theologian. It originated as part of the final chapters of my PhD dissertation for the theology department at Fordham University on "The Ideas of Power and Freedom in the Theology of Paul Tillich" (1976). The third essay was delivered at Villanova University at the annual convention of the College Theology Society in 2000. It offers a contribution to Buddhist and Christian dialogue on the subject of self-emptying. It was published in *The Journal of Pastoral Counseling* of Iona College, in 2000. The "Self-Emptying of Christ and the Christian" thus represents research from four decades on the theme of kenosis or self-emptying.

One reason to collect, edit, and publish these essays now is represented by a series of questions. Did the original meaning for the self-emptying of Christ imply, (1) God's generosity in creation, (2) the Incarnation, (3) Christ's death for us on the Cross, (4) all of the above? Do Christians today practice self-emptying? What is the object of self-emptying? What are similar or related Christian practices? Is the current interest in "servant leadership," as a model in contemporary church and culture, related to the self-emptying servant of Philippians 2? Does the practice of self-emptying contribute to our present secular age? Does it imply deconstructing the content of Christian faith and morals in contemporary culture? These and related questions are examined in the course of this collection. They constitute a heuristic ground or cluster of questions that challenge Christians today and seek elaboration as we proceed to explain the meaning of kenosis or "emptying" in its ancient and modern contexts.

The Second Vatican Council, which met in Rome for four years, 1962–65, provided the original background for this research. The sixties are symbolic in American memories for our national engagement in the Vietnam civil war, the anti-war protest, the civil-rights movement, and public anxieties accelerated by the assassinations of President John F. Kennedy, Rev. Martin Luther King Jr., and Bobby Kennedy. Vatican II now seems small and far away in American memories after almost half a century, but it was one of the greatest councils in the history of the Catholic Church. It was also one of the largest gatherings of representatives of world Christianity.

The Council was about to begin its third session when I began four years of immersion in theology. Many aspects of theology were touched by the council process which resulted in sixteen documents. Three major changes stand out for their immediate impact during my initial encounter with theology: changes in (1) liturgy, (2) study of Scripture, and (3) ecumenism. The study of Philippians 2:5–11 presented here was composed in the context of a worldwide, Catholic renewal of interest in Scripture precipitated by Vatican II. The return to scriptural sources is connected with renewal in liturgy and the ecumenical movement fostered by Vatican II.

The ecumenical movement had an immediate effect on Alma College, which the California Province of the Society of Jesus had acquired in 1934 as a place to educate theologians on their way to ordination and future ministries in the Catholic Church. I graduated one year before Alma College moved, in 1969, from the redwood-forested foothills of the Santa Cruz Mountains to Berkeley, California, adjacent to the University of California, where it would continue as the Jesuit School of Theology at Berkeley, one of the nine associate schools of the Graduate Theological Union. Forty years later, in 2009, it realigned itself once again, and changed its name to the Jesuit School of Theology of Santa Clara University. It is one of only two remaining Jesuit theologates in the U.S. The other is Weston School of Theology at Boston College. Both schools also prepare lay people for theology and ministry.

In the fall of 1966, Fr. Ben F. Meyer, SJ, (1927–95), an assistant professor of fundamental theology at Alma College, had just returned from Europe with his PhD, and special study with Joachim Jeremias. Ben organized a seminar on the "Servant of Yahweh" for student theologians. Four of us took the seminar, which began with nine meetings and ended with a tutorial on a specific topic, related to the seminar, chosen by each student.

The seminar began with a study of the four servant songs in Second Isaiah, concentrating on the fourth song of Is 52:13—53:12, called the song of the "suffering servant." Our research included analysis of the original Hebrew vocabulary, and the textual variants in the Septuagint (LXX,) the Hexapla, and Palestinian Targums with questions about the identity of the servant. Then we investigated all New Testament references to Jesus as the servant, looking for the Isaian servant motifs in Acts, Pauline literature, 1 Peter, Hebrews, the Synoptics, and John. Special attention was given to the eucharistic words of Jesus.

Ironically, the focus of my research, the Philippians hymn of 2:5–11, did not contain the altruistic, expiatory, or vicarious atonement language prominent in the "suffering servant" of Isaiah, who suffered "for us" and "for our sins." But it had sufficient continuity with the theme of the seminar, the "Servant of God," to be acceptable. I titled the study, "The Gospel Writ Small: Toward A Theology of Philippians 2:5–11." It was presented for seminar discussion in February, 1967. It was submitted to Ben Meyer and the Alma faculty to fulfill requirements for the Master of Sacred Theology degree, which was awarded in 1968. Strangely, my transcript for that year lacks the title of Ben Meyer's servant seminar. After the heading "seminar," the transcript prints the title of my research paper as above. Ben Meyer's seminar title is missing.

The second essay requires an explanation of my interest in Paul Tillich. The essay is one-third of the fourth and last chapter of the longer PhD dissertation on "The Ideas of Power and Freedom in the Theology of Paul Tillich," completed at Fordham University, NY, in 1976.

The first time I heard of Paul Tillich was as an adversary for Scholastic theses in metaphysics during my philosophy studies (1958–61) for the master's degree at Mount St. Michael's College, the Jesuit school of philosophy, an adjunct of Gonzaga University, Spokane, Washington. The Society of Jesus was suppressed by popes from 1773 to 1814. To that extent it lacked a scholarly heritage that directly engaged the Enlightenment and Romantic rise of interest in Transcendental Subjectivity in European thought during that forty-one year hiatus, a heritage provided by Friedrich Schelling (1775–1854) and Paul Tillich (1886–1965).

Professor Gene Bianchi noted my shortcomings when I interpreted Tillich's *The Courage To Be* for his course on "Contemporary Protestant Theology" at the University of San Francisco in 1966. At Fordham's graduate program in theology, Avery Dulles allowed me to examine Tillich's views for his course on "Faith and Reason" in the spring of 1970. At that time I was fortunate to audit Tom F. Driver's course on Paul Tillich at Union Theological Seminary. I also researched Tillich, among other scholars, for "Contemporary Christology," a seminar directed by Doris Donnelly.

By then I had read many of Tillich's books and sermons and considered him a valuable resource and partner for the Catholic and Protestant ecumenical dialogues that flourished after Vatican Council II. One of my teachers at Alma College, Daniel O'Hanlon, SJ, wrote his STD dissertation, guided by Gustave Weigel, SJ, at the Gregorian University in Rome, on "The Influence of Schelling on the Thought of Paul Tillich" (1957). Both Weigel and O'Hanlon were active in ecumenical dialogue.

My mind was set to pursue research on Tillich after I was asked to host Jerald Brauer, dean of the Divinity School of the University of Chicago, when he came to visit St. Thomas Aquinas College, Sparkill, NY in 1973 and Dominican College, Blauvelt, NY in 1974. At that time I taught at both colleges. Brauer had hired Tillich to teach at the divinity school as the last chapter (1962–65) in Tillich's long American academic career. I did some more crash reading, and Julio Burunat and I had some wonderful conversations with Dean Brauer about the work of his friend and colleague, "Paulus."

During the 1970s, Tillich's two dissertations on Schelling were published in English translation by Victor Nuovo. At that time I discovered that Walter Kasper, a leader in Catholic ecumenical work, published a German study of Schelling that explained his kenotic theory. Just as my thesis engaged Schelling's influence on Tillich's ideas of power and freedom, and myth and symbol in the history of revelation, so the second essay printed here, on "Tillich's Kenotic Tendency," explains how Tillich's ideas of Christ as the New Being who overcomes estrangement, and empowers our weakened, finite freedom, has a foundation in Schelling's kenotic theory.

The third essay on "Self-Emptying in Christian and Buddhist Spirituality" grew out of publications that traced many U.S. professional collegiate conversations with Masao Abe, a Zen Buddhist scholar who seemed to wear the mantle of D. T. Suzuki (d. 1966), as the leading proponent of the Kyoto school of Zen Buddhism in Japan. I had taught world religions for many years, so I thought an essay that compared the teaching of the "*Heart Sūtra*" about *Śūnyatā* ("nothing") with the emptying or kenosis of the Philippians hymn would contribute to this discussion. I presented it at the annual convention of the College Theology Society at Villanova University in the spring of 2000. Barbara Socor, a colleague at Dominican College, forwarded the paper to the *Journal of Pastoral Counseling* at Iona College, which published it later in 2000.

One might legitimately ask how a "thick" historical and literary analysis of the Christian-Buddhist comparison on this one topic contributes to spirituality. A similar question might be asked, about how the previous two essays contribute to theology. The solution belongs to inquiries into the many tasks that are called forward to fulfill the exercises we call theology. In the last analysis, my appeal is to the method of theology proposed by Bernard Lonergan. Just as the works of Karl Rahner emboldened me to reach further to engage the post-Kantian, existential, and German-romantic-idealist thought of Paul Tillich, so the multiple inductive and deductive tasks that operate in the intentional consciousness of theological method prepare one's research to enter into a wide conversation about the operations of human understanding that engage the mystery of God communicating among us. Sharing our humble insights about that mystery that lives among us is at the core of theology and spirituality.

It should be noted that when composing the second and third essays, I conducted some additional research on Philippians 2, and the kenosis/self-emptying theme. Kenosis references have taken many alternative routes since this biblical research began in the mid-1960s. Additional recent research on the hymn to Christ of Phil 2:5–11 is contained as an Update section at the end of the first essay. The critical notes for Part I were reduced from 166 to 19 for this collection; moving in-text citations to the notes, however, brought the total back to 165. Similarly, for Part II, the Tillich essay, the comment notes were reduced from 50 to 18 for this publication; changing the in-text cites to notes increased the final total to 51. For any stray errors (from the Latin *errare,* to wander), whether of content or format, I take full responsibility.

The Hymn—Philippians 2:5–11

5 **Think this way among yourselves that also is in Christ Jesus**
Touto phroneite en hymin ho kai en Christō Iēsou

6 a **who though he was in the form of God**
hos en morphē Theou hyparchōn

b **did not regard as something to be grasped**
ouch harpagmon hēgēsato

c **his equality with God**
to einai isa Theō

7 a **but emptied himself**
alla heauton ekenōsen

b **taking the form of a servant**
morphēn doulou labōn

c **becoming like other humans**
en homoiōmati anthrōpōn genomenos

d **and in appearance found as a human**
kai schēmati heuretheis hōs anthrōpos

8 a **he humbled himself**
etapeinōsen heauton

b **becoming obedient**
genomenos hypēkoos

c **even to death**
mechri thanatou

d **death on the cross.**
thanatou de staurou.

9 a **Therefore God greatly exalted him**
dio kai ho Theos auton hyperypsōsen

b **and bestowed on him the name**
kai echarisato autō to onoma

c **above every other name**
to hyper pan onoma

10 a **that at the name of Jesus**
hina en tō onomati Iēsou

b **every knee should bend**
pan gony kampsē

c **in heaven, on earth, and in the underworld**
epouraniōn kai epigeiōn kai katachthoniōn

11 a **and every tongue should confess**
kai pasa glōssa exomologēsetai

b **that Jesus Christ is LORD**
hoti Kyrios Iēsous Christos

c **to the glory of God the Father.**
eis doxan Theou Patros.

Part I

A Theology of Philippians 2:5–11

INTRODUCTION

This paper does not attempt to pioneer a new position on the famed christological passage of Philippians 2:5–11. It aims rather to assess the evidence offered in an already large and varied literature on the topic, in order to make considered judgments about its genre, structure, language, authorship, exegesis, and theology. It is the writer's hope that this detailed study will not discourage readers, but will rather enhance their receptivity to the Gospel. For these few lines contain the Gospel writ small; they condense and celebrate the central story of Christ.

GENRE

An immediate question arises, how to define the literary type of Phil 2:6–11. First of all, is it prose or poetry? The distinction between the two is, in general, less sharp in biblical literature than in the later literature of the West. But the convergence of numerous characteristics of poetry, e.g., strophic structure, parallelisms, and meter, to be treated in more detail below, leads us to acknowledge that we are dealing here with poetry. The question is: what kind of poetry? A text from Colossians appears to offer some possibilities:

> Let the word of Christ dwell in you richly as you teach and admonish one another in all wisdom, and as you sing psalms, hymns, and spiritual songs with thankfulness in your hearts to God. (3:16)

Do we have in the Philippians hymn one or the other of the three different categories of poetry, psalms, hymns, and spiritual songs (Greek, *ōidē*) mentioned in Colossians?

Other than in Col 3:16 and the parallel in Eph 5:19, the Greek word *ōidē* is mentioned only in Rev 5:9; 14:3; 15:3. Singing hymns is mentioned elsewhere, in the account of the departure from the last supper Mark 14:26 || Matt 26:30 and in Acts 16:25 as well as Heb 2:12. Psalm singing is mentioned more frequently, usually in reference to the quite general classification of the liturgical poetry of the OT.

In the parallel passage in Eph 5:16, conjunctions separate the three types. But is this enough evidence to support a strict distinction between the three? Probably not; and there is no further evidence to illuminate the question. We will refer to our text, then, as a "hymn," but without meaning to distinguish it thereby from "psalm" or "ode."

Is it a liturgical hymn? We know from the extra-biblical witness of Pliny in his reply to Trajan that the Christians assembled on special days in the early dawn and recited songs among themselves to Christ as to God.[1] This description refers apparently to a liturgical assembly. The full account[2] seems to include a morning

1. Pliny to Trajan, AD 112 [*Epistularum ad Traianum liber 10*, 96]: "They (the Christians) insisted, however, that their whole crime or error came to this: they had the custom of meeting on a certain fixed day, before daybreak, to sing a hymn, alternating among themselves, to Christ as God; and to bind themselves solemnly by an oath, not with any criminal intent, but to avoid all fraud, theft, adultery, unfaithfulness to their promises, or denial of 'the deposit' if summoned to do so. After dispatching this business, it was their habit to disband, reassembling once more to take food, which is, however, of an ordinary and innocent kind . . ." Stanley, *Apostolic Church in New Testament*, 98–99.

2. Ibid., 99.

baptismal liturgy and a reassembling for an evening Eucharist.[3] The most notable item is the christological character of the songs.

When one raises the question whether a particular NT passage is connected with the liturgy, it is important to place this smaller inquiry within the broad context of all the New Testament. Except for some personally directed letters like 1 & 2 Timothy, 1 Titus, Philemon, and 3 John, it seems most likely that the major corpus of gospels and letters were written for Christian communities and intended to be proclaimed or recited in gatherings whose purpose was the worship of God. In this larger sense all of the NT is liturgical. As a letter written to, and to be read to, all the community, the whole of Philippians is liturgical.

With our limited evidence, to what extent can we identify particular NT hymns with an early liturgical setting? After all, when Paul and Silas sang and were overheard by their fellow prisoners, they were in a rather poor liturgical situation—prison (Acts 16:25). The Apocalypse (Revelation) and Hebrews, on the other hand, offer several indications of liturgical singing. The remarks about singing in 1 Cor 14:15, 26 and Jas 5:13 likewise suggest a liturgical context. Moreover, if the celebration of the Eucharist retained the structure of the Jewish paschal rite, the first half of the *Hallel*, Pss 113 and 114, would be sung before taking the second cup of blessing. Before going out to the garden, Jesus and the eleven probably sang the paschal *Hallel*, or the second half of it. Many consider the "praising" of Acts 2:46–47 also belongs in the context of an Eucharistic gathering. However it is not so much a

3. Boismard, *Quatre Hymnes Baptismales*, 173; "*On rejoin les constatations faites à propos des hymnes de 1 Petr 1, 3–5 et 2, 22–24. Des lors, une conclusion s'impose: lorsque saint Paul écrit aux fidèles de Rome, il utilize les mêmes materiaux de la liturgie et de la catéchèse baptismale que l'auteur de la Prima Petri. Ce fait ne doit pas nous étonner outré mésure. Paul écrit en effet a une église qu'il n'a pas évangélisée personnellement, qu'il ne connaît donc pas. Pour être sur de parler le même langage que ses lecteurs, la solution la plus simple était de développer des thèmes connus de tous, parce qu'ils faisaient le fond de la liturgie et de la catéchèse baptismale: "Ignorez-vous donc que . . . sachant bien que . . .sachant que . . .*" (Rom 6:3, 6, 9).

question whether the liturgy is hymnic, which no one would question, but whether or not biblical hymns were originally liturgical.

Boismard has analyzed the structure of four hymns in 1 Peter. He concludes that St. Paul in Romans 6 uses the same liturgical and baptismal catechetical material as the author of 1 Pet 3. This same author has done considerable work on the parabolic hymnic structure of St. John's prologue.[4] With studies such as these, one is not surprised to find a distinctive hymn and perhaps a liturgical hymn in a particular NT writing.

Several other passages in the NT are generally identified as hymns. Some of these are more obvious than others. The ordinary reader will immediately recognize the canticles of Mary, the Angel Gabriel, Zachary, and Simeon in the Lukan infancy narrative. The beatitudes according to Matthew are uniquely structured to at least border on the hymnic. Sections of the Apocalypse (Revelation) and of the letter to the Hebrews are considered by many as hymns. However, in the Pauline corpus hymns are more concealed. Paul's rhetorical prose style constantly bursts into parallels that border on the hymnic. Some sections commonly pointed out include: 1 Tim 3:16; 2 Tim 2:12–13; Titus 3:4–7; Col 1:15–20; Eph 1:3–14.

Several questions arise concerning this phenomenon in Paul's writing. Does Paul compose hymns? Or are these sections pre-existing compositions by an anonymous Christian writer, or by several within the community? Were they originally liturgical? If liturgical, did they originate in Hellenistic Christian churches or in Jewish Christian assemblies? Finally, can liturgical hymns be distinguished from creeds, confessions, and doxologies?

To the first question we suggest a fairly strong affirmative answer. But if Boismard's hypothesis is correct, Paul also incorporates pre-existing liturgical pieces into his letters.[5] Finally, Pauline hymns are often introduced or concluded with confession to the

4. Boismard, *St. John's Prologue.*

5. Boismard, *Quatre Hymnes Baptismales*, 173; Hunter, *Paul*, 36–44, 122–26.

Lordship of Jesus, and an accompanying praise of God's wonderful power manifested toward humanity in Jesus.

Perhaps the clearest approach to the Philippians hymn is to begin with the second half, 2:9–11, which some consider to be modeled on an ancient enthronement celebration. Joachim Jeremias says:

> The ancient coronation ritual exemplified for us in the ancient Egyptian ritual, consisted of three actions: 1. the Elevation; 2. the Presentation or Proclamation; 3. the Enthronement of the new king. This triple-action form of coronation hymn occurs in the New Testament not only in 1 Tim 3:16, but also elsewhere, for example, in Phil. 2:9–11 (1. Elevation in v. 9a; 2. Proclamation of the Name above every name in v. 9b; 3. Homage to the Enthroned one by gesture and confession v. 10–11.)[6]

Some liturgical songs of the OT, employ a similar structure of the enthronement festival to celebrate Yahweh in terms of some "new exodus," or "new creation."[7] Some authors suggest the triple-action coronation occurs in other places in the NT, Matt 28:18–20; Heb 1:5–14. This action is related to the bestowal of Lordship on Jesus who has been raised up. In this sense it recalls the frequently employed Ps 110:1 and 8:6; cf. Acts 2:33; 5:31; 7:56; Rom 8:34; 1 Cor 15:25; Eph 1:20; Col 3:1.

> This enthronement theme, which provided such a popular vehicle for the expression of Christ's divinity (cf. Rom 1:4),

6. Jeremias, *Promise to the Nations*, 47–48. Jeremias refers to Käsemann, '*Kritische Analyse von Phil*', 346 ff. Stanley uses the same conclusion rightly adding reference to Babylonian culture in *Apostolic Church in New Testament*, 110. The conjecture of the presence of such a festival in the OT reflected in the Psalms has been proposed by the Scandinavian school (e.g., Mowinckel, Johnson, Bentzen). To read this triple enthronement into the Monarchic period may only be a hypothesis. This would be true also of post-exilic Israel unless some correlation with a Babylonian practice is shown. Thus the evidence for this triple-action in NT hymns may not be very solid. Cf. Ap-Thomas, "Appreciation of Mowinckel," 315–25.

7. Bentzen, *Introduction to Old Testament*, 163.

> was employed in two ways: to describe Christ's eschatological function as "Judge of the living and the dead" (Acts 10:42) or to portray Christ's actual role as Saviour, exercised by His intercession in heaven (Rom 8:34; Heb 7:25), or His intervention in this world through the Spirit (Acts 3:26).[8]

J. Jervell,[9] E. Käsemann,[10] and A. Seeberg think the hymn in Phil 2 originates with a baptismal liturgy because: (1) there is a connection between confession of Jesus as Lord with the baptismal confession, (2) the victory of Jesus over the spirits is designated by the three-storied universe, (3) Baptism was administered "in the name of Jesus," and (4) the word "form" in the first half of the hymn may be related to the "conformation" of the Christian to Christ in Baptism. J. Hering[11] and A. M. Hunter[12] think it came from a Eucharistic liturgy at Antioch. E. Lohmeyer thinks it was originally sung at the Eucharistic liturgy of Jerusalem.[13] D. Stanley suggests it originated in the same circle that carried and spread the Deutero-Isaiah Christology in Jerusalem, was learned by Paul at Antioch, was used by him in his early catechizing at Philippi, and finally was recalled in the letter to the Philippians.[14] Lohmeyer would seem to have landed on the most accurate reconstruction of the *Sitz im Leben* of the hymn. The supporting theological reason is the substrata of early *ebed*, servant Christology underlying the gospel *didachē*, which is most evident in the early formulas in Acts.[15]

8. Stanley, *Apostolic Church in New Testament*, 108.

9. Jervell, *Imago Dei*, 205–8.

10. Käsemann, '*Kritische Analyse von Phil*,' 47; cf. Feuillet, "*l'Hymne christologique*," 488. Cf. also R. Martin, *Early Christian Confession*, 12–13, 40.

11. R. Martin, *Early Christian Confession*, 43 fn. 21.

12. Hunter, *Paul and His Predecessors*, 42.

13. Lohmeyer, *Kyrios Jesus*, 66.

14. Stanley, *Apostolic Church in New Testament*, 350.

15. Hunter, *Paul and His Predecessors*, 142, fn. 1: "Here I should mention Cullmann's suggestion that 'Paidology' may have been something characteristically Petrine. Note that, of the four places in the NT where Jesus

When we refer to the Philippians hymn as "christological," we are supported in this designation by the description of the hymn singing in the passages in Col and Eph. However, this is not to ignore the fact that the christological hymns are always theocentric. Both passages relate the singing *through* Christ and *to* the Father:

> . . . be filled with the Spirit, as you sing psalms and hymns and spiritual songs among yourselves, singing and making melody to the Lord in your hearts, giving thanks to God the Father at all times and for everything in the name of our Lord Jesus Christ (Eph 5:18b–20).

> Let the word of Christ dwell in you richly: teach and admonish one another in all wisdom; and with gratitude in your hearts sing psalms, hymns and spiritual songs to God. And whatever you do, in word or deed, do everything in the name of the Lord Jesus, giving thanks to God the Father through him (Col 3:16–17).

The singing in these contexts is understood as done *in* the name of the Lord, *to* the Father. Both elicit the attitude of thanksgiving. Inasmuch as the entire movement of redemption originates with the Father and returns to the Father, a song to Christ as redeemer is a hymn in praise of the Father.[16] The fact that the Philippians hymn, whose subject is Christ, is also directed to the glory of the Father can be seen from the concluding verse, and also from the relation of the Father to Christ in 2:6 and 2:9.

When Paul says, "Let the word of Christ dwell in you richly" (Col 3:16), in the context of this song-making, he seems to be indi-

---

is called *pais Theou,* two are in Peter's speeches and two in prayers made in his presence. Next, remember how, at Caesarea Philippi, Jesus had been compelled to read Peter a stern lesson about the necessity of the Son of Man's suffering. Then observe that it is in 1 Pet 2 that Jesus is identified with the Servant more fully than anywhere else in the NT. Finally, note how prominent the doctrine of *Ebed Yahweh* appears in Mark's Gospel which, according to tradition, reflects the preaching of Peter. Did the man who had originally recoiled in horror at the idea of a suffering Messiah, live to set it at the center of his preaching because he knew how much store his Master set by it?"

16. Stanley, *Apostolic Church in New Testament*, 98.

cating that somehow the community which is the body of Christ, when engaged in communal music and worship, is the voice of Christ, uttering the words of Christ which dwell within them.[17]

STRUCTURE AND LANGUAGE

Whether Phil 2:6–11 was originally composed in Greek or in a Semitic language may be unanswerable.[18] In any case, its technique as well as its substance is to be understood against a biblical background. The most distinguishing characteristic of biblical Hebrew poetry is its parallelism.[19]

The kinds of parallels common in the OT may be reduced to three: synonymous, antithetical, and synthetic, introduced by Bishop Robert Lowth's study of Hebrew poetry in 1753. Synonymous parallel repeats and reinforces the first line of a verse with a second couplet with the same corresponding idea being echoed in the same or equivalent sense as the first line, though in different terms.[20] Antithetical parallel contrasts the terms of the second line with those of the first, as in Prov 10:1. Synthetic or constructive parallel, employs the second line to supplement and complete the thought of the first; it may partly repeat and partly build upon the first line as in Ps 2:6. C. F. Burney distinguishes a special aspect about the first and third type and adds a fourth, climactic, which adds something more than an echo of the first line and completes the sense of the distich thus forming as it were its

17. Ibid., 96.

18. For Hebrew see Delitzsch, *Hebrew New Testament*; for Aramaic version, see R. Martin, "Form-analysis of Philippians," 613–14, fn. 2; also Clarke, *New Testament Problems*, 148.

19. The phenomenon of parallelism may account for the label *mashal* or "likeness" which is applied to verses in the OT. The term *mashal* has a wider extension than just a sentence or proverb; it also refers to an enigmatic comparison requiring interpretation, Bentzen, *Introduction to Old Testament*, 167. Nelis, "Poetry," 1168–77.

20. Note the antiquity of synonymous parallelism from Ugaritic in Dahood, *Psalms I 1–50*, xxxiii ff. The examples cited are in Bright, *Jeremiah*, cxxv–cxxxv III. Ps. 24:3.

climax.[21] For example, Ps 23:4: "Though I walk in the dark valley/ I fear no harm, for you are with me."[22] Parabolic and comparative variations of these three basic types have been suggested, but they seem conveniently reducible to the types mentioned above.[23]

Another structural element, which is related to the poetic use of parallelism, consists in the construction of groups of parallels in formal combinations. Such a period or verse is made of two, less often of three, *stichoi* or *cola* (sense-lines). "The unit of Hebrew poetry is the *stichos* or line."[24] Depending upon the parallelism employed, these progressive additions can often create a "stairlike" or climactic effect. This is the building type of parallelism which Burney introduced as a fourth type.[25]

A second distinguishing feature of biblical poetry is the tone-color which is the effect of sound combinations. There is a notable absence of rhyme in Hebrew poetry, but there is assonance. This recurrence of identical sounds on emphatic words may be created by pronominal suffixes or verbal endings. These are occasionally placed at the end of verse members to approximate rhyme. However this particular sound-feature is considered "far too uncommon to be characteristic."[26]

More frequent is the play on words.

> Alliteration, assonance, and paronomasia, the latter including not only the pun proper but word-play in general, the

21. Burney, *Poetry of Our Lord*.

22. McKenzie, *Dictionary of the Bible*, 680.

23. Bentzen, *Introduction to Old Testament*, 173.

24. McKenzie, *Dictionary of the Bible*, 680.

25. When the elements within a line are lettered, one can see the many combinations. "As the fire ignites the forest, as the flame sets—blaze the hills," (Ps. 83:15) is an ABC/ABC combination. But one of these elements could be incomplete: ABC/BC or ABC/AB, and often a new element, "D" is added as compensation: ABC/BCD or ABCD/ABEF/ABEG (Ps. 29:1 ff), "This arrangement, incidentally, is paralleled in Canaanite (Ugaritic) literature, from which Psalm 29 seems originally to have been adapted." Bright, *Jeremiah*, cxxx.

26. Ibid., cxxviii; e.g., Deut 6:7 in Hebrew.

> opposition and juxtaposition of similar sounding words, are characteristic features of all early poetry; they are especially prominent in the poetry of the Semites . . .[27]

The poetry of the Bible is unlike Western poetry in numerous respects. It does not make use of Greek rhythmic movements with numerical and quantitative accents like iambic, trochaic, etc. It does employ a proclitic type of ascending accent. Accent plus content determine the divisions of lines into *cola* of two or three, and sometimes four rhythmic units or beats. Each primary word is usually taken to merit the value of one beat. Thus the rhythmic units are rather short. However, we approach this with caution for, "[T]he whole subject of Hebrew meter is beset with unsolved problems, upon which there is the widest disagreement among scholars."[28] In the NT,

> We have no infallible criteria enabling us to pronounce such and such a passage a hymn in the strictest sense of the word, i.e., something sung by a Christian congregation as an act of worship. A metrical test is impossible: metrical verse in Christian hymnology came much later; e.g., Papyrus Oxyrhynchus, 1786, contains a Christian hymn of the third century, written in anapestic meter, and complete with musical notes.[29]

Finally, the contribution of *Gattungsgeschichte*, the German term for the history of the classification of literary forms, has

27. Black, *Aramaic Approach to Gospels*, 118; e.g., Is 5:7; 10:15; 27:12; 32:14; 51:6; Jer 1:11; 48:2; Amos 8:1–3; a good example is also Deut 6:7 in Hebrew.

28. Perhaps we can compare it with the sprung rhythm of G. M. Hopkins. Bright, *Jeremiah*, cxxvii. Bright considers accent as one of two major aspects of Hebrew poetry. "The characteristic marks of Hebrew poetry are essentially two: parallelism of members, as Lowth was the first to see; and the (more or less) regular recurrence of accented syllables within the individual members" (cxxvii). The uncertainty comes from: 1) how the words were actually pronounced, 2) whether accented syllables alone are determinative, or 3) whether accent alternates, including both accented and unaccented syllables.

29. Hunter, *Paul and His Predecessors*, 37.

helped scholars identify the enthronement section of Phil 2:9–11 that we mentioned above. In the first half of the hymn some other elements of the OT hymn form also seem to be evident, as we shall point out presently.

If we approach the Philippians hymn from the viewpoint of biblical poetry we discover several characteristics in the use of (1) parallelism, (2) assonance, (3) hymn forms, and (4) meter/accent. The poetic structure and language is determined by the original Greek text. (To assist comprehension, an English translation follows Greek vocabulary and phrases when they are first used.)

1. *Parallelism*. There is abundant use of parallelism on the level of single words, phrases, and whole lines which determines the thought content and contributes to the structure and meaning of the Philippians hymn. In the first half, (1) *ouch*/"not" and *alla*/"but," set off contrasting antitheses.[30] (2) *En morphē Theou hyparchōn*/"existing in the form of God" || *morphē doulou labōn*/"taking the form of a servant," employ *morphē*/"form" in synonymous parallel and word order, while repeated use of the participle creates an additional parallel sound value. But there is a strong antithesis between *Theou*/"God" and *doulou*/"servant." *Theou* looks ahead to the contrasting phrases using *anthrōpos*/"human," and the contrast is repeated in another form with *isa Theō*/"like God" and its antithesis *hōs anthrōpos*/"human." Finally, *doulou*/"servant" looks far ahead to the antithesis *Kyrios*/"Lord" in the climax of the hymn. Thus the opening verse sets up the remaining antitheses in the first half of the hymn. (3) The prepositional phrase *en morphē*/"in the form" is set against the phrase *en homoiōmati*/"in the likeness," and actually admits of a closer synonymous parallel in word order than exists between the single phrase *morphē doulou labōn*/"taking the form of a servant." It also directly contrasts *Theou*/"God" and *anthrōpōn*/"human." (4) *morphēn doulou labōn, en homoiōmati anthrōpōn genomenos, kai schēmati heuretheis hōs anthrōpos, etapeinōsen heauton genomenos hypēkoos*/"taking the

30. Zerwick, *Biblical Greek*, 150.

form of a servant, becoming like other humans, and found in appearance as a human, he humbled himself becoming obedient," use synonymous parallel by repeating participles in a building way, and add new elements to each phrase which produce a climactic effect. (5) *Heauton ekenōsen*/"he emptied himself" || *etapeinōsen heauton*/"he humbled himself," both employ the reflexive adjective in a chiastic word order and build upon the meaning of the verbs. (6) *Morphē*/"form," *homoiōmati*/"likeness," and *schēmati*/"appearance" are three words that refer to perceptions. Add the *ouch . . . isa Theō*/"not . . . equal to God" with *hōs anthrōpos*/"as a human," and the poem has constructed the portrait and quality of person in a running synthetic parallel. (7) *Mechri thanatou, thanatou de staurou*/"even to death, death on the cross" climax the first part of the hymn with strong synthetic parallelism.

In the second half of the hymn the strong parallelism is not so evident, but the whole piece moves in a progressive building toward the climax. The first half employed a strong paratactic structure, like the Aramaicism in Mark's Gospel 10:33–34, which links the parallels by using *ouch*/"not," *alla*/"but," and *kai*/"and." The second half, while using the coordinating *kai* four times, more significantly subordinates modifying phrases with *hoti*/"that" and *hina*/"that."[31] This section is introduced with a phrase similar to Is 52:13, and continues with a description of the homage which is given to Jesus, modeled on Is 45:23. (1) *Dio kai ho Theos auton hyperypsōsen* || *kai echarisato autō* employ verbs in synthetic parallel with the pronoun in chiastic positions parallel to the reflexive *heauton* used above. (2) *Echarisato autō to onoma* || *to hyper pan onoma* || *hina en tō onomati* . . . builds upon the repetition of "name." (3) *Pan onoma* || *pan gony* || *pasa glōssa* build upon the idea of universality. (4) The universality is further emphasized by the triple storied universe, *epouraniōn kai epigeiōn kai katachthoniōn*. (5) The name *Iēsou* is contrasted with the name *Kyrios*. (6) *Pan gony kampsē* and *pasa glōssa exomologēsetai* complete the full expression of homage

31. Black, *Aramaic Approach to Gospels*, 43.

in a building parallel. It is in the light of these parallels that one is most strongly aware of the poetry of this hymn.

2. *Assonance*. Woven within these parallels is a frequent occurrence of words with similar sounds as well as words repeated. This creates the poetic quality of assonance. The words repeated are: *Theos, morphē, anthropōs, genomenos, heautos, autos, pan, onoma*, *Iēsou,* and *hyper* (as a prefix and as a preposition). The words contributing to the assonance are the words that end in *-ma* or *-mati: homoiōmati, schēmati* in the first part, and the *onoma* forms in the second half. Also contributing to the tone of the first half are the verbs ending in "n" and the long vowel sounds, both of which create a drawn out musical quality when spoken.

3. *Hymn forms*. Some possible uses of hymn-forms might include the transitional *phroneite* (v. 5), which is like the OT hymn introduction employing an imperative directed to the believing community (Pss 150 and 119).[32] Also occurring in OT poetry is the transition to the body of the hymn by means of a relative pronoun which we have in *hos* (v. 6) (Pss 16:7; 31:8; 66:20; 124:6). The use of participles in apposition describing the power and other qualities of Yahweh in OT poetry, called "predicative style," could also influence the five participial constructions in the first half of the hymn (Pss 9:12; 136:3; 144:1).

4. *Meter/accent*. Finally, to evaluate the hymn in terms of accent presents difficulties. Just what is to be taken as having primary accent is not clear. The number of accented syllables per unit or colon may be two, three or four. Accented units constituting a series of parallel members should not be grouped without regard for their thought-content. This involves some preliminary theological interpretation, which may or may not be verified by the structure. The goal in this task is to find that structure which most adequately conforms with the meaning of the parallel verse members.

32. Bentzen, *Introduction to Old Testament*.

In a classic study, four divisions of the hymn have been offered by Ernst Lohmeyer in 1928,[33] Lucien Cerfaux in 1954, Joachim Jeremias in 1963, and André Feuillet in 1965. (See Table 1 for a comparison of these four structural analyses.) The progressive development by reason of these respective studies has resulted in a growing acceptance of the following points: (1) in general there is some kind of balance between the form and content; (2) Pauline additions to the pre-existing hymn have upset the balance of the structure.

Many authors still accept Lohmeyer's divisions of two strophes of six balanced versus, three in the first half and three in the second half, each containing three lines apiece, and each line balanced in a 3:3:3 beat (Beare, Benoit, Martin, Stanley, Feuillet). Cerfaux and Jeremias agree that the hymn should be divided into three strophes, not two, and that the division within the first half of the hymn between strophe I and II should begin with *en homoiōmati* since it is parallel in structure and thought with the opening *en morphē*, etc. This differs from the "'common opinion' which would begin the second main sentence with *kai schēmati*."[34] Cerfaux and Jeremias differ regarding stanza III and regarding Pauline glosses. Cerfaux does not seem to attempt to balance the lines in his three-part division. Jeremias suggests a four line arrangement within each part and considers *thanatou de staurou* (with Lohmeyer), *epouraniōn kai epigeiōn kai katachthoniōn,* and *eis doxan Theou Patros* as Pauline glosses. Thus the hymn has a I || II+III structure similar to Rom 1:22–32.[35]

33. Lohmeyer, *Kyrios Jesus*, suggests that the hymn has a 3:3:3 rhythm. "In fact we can show that the 3:3:3 form, exceptional in the OT, was apparently the favourite form of the early Church. An obvious parallel is Eph. 5:14." Also 1 Tim. 3:16, Luke. 2:29–32..." May we not suppose that the Philippians hymn and the *Nunc Dimittis* have the same origin, both having been composed in Aramaic in the early Church at Jerusalem and speedily translated into Greek for the Greek-speaking members of the bilingual community?" (Clarke, *New Testament Problems*, 146–47.) Also Lohmeyer, *Briefe an die Philipper*.

34. Cerfaux, *Christ in St. Paul*, 383.

35. Jeremias, "*Zu Phil 2.7*," 188.

We shall treat the question of Pauline authorship in the following pages. While there may certainly be more than one Pauline gloss, Jeremias seems to offer an extreme solution to the problem of the hymn-form, which he resolves in favor of balance at the cost of unity.

Setting out to determine the structure, Feuillet arrived at a division of two strophes, each with three two-lined members. To achieve this he strongly suggests that all of verse eight is a Pauline repetition of verse seven, and therefore probably a gloss.[36]

Table 1. Four Structural Analyses of Philippians 2:6–11

Lohmeyer (1928)		Cerfaux (1954)		Jeremias (1963)		Feuillet (1965)	
I	6 a	I	6 a	I	6 a	I	6 a
	b		b c		b c		b c
	c						
II	7 a		7 a		7 a		7 a
	b		b		b		b
	c	II	c	II	c		c
III	d		d		d		d
	8 a		8 a		8 a		8 (a b)
	b c (d)		b c (d)		b c (d)		(c d)
IV	9 a	III	9 a	III	9 a	II	9 a
	b		b c		b c		b c
	c						
V	10 a		10 a		10 a b (c)		10 a b
	b		b (c)				c
	c						
VI	11 a		11 a b (c)		11 a b (c)		11 a
	b						b c
	c						

( ) stands for Pauline gloss

36. Feuillet, "*L'Hymne*."

Related to the question of structure is the problem of whether the hymn is an examle of *Heilsgeschichte in Hymnenform*, "salvation history in hymn form," like John's prologue. These "differ from all the other hymns in the New Testament, in that they relate, narrate and preach the story of Christ."[37] It is "the oldest document on which the whole Christology of the later times, especially the doctrine of the three stages of Christ's existence, was built up."[38] If the three strophes of the hymn stand for Christ's pre-existence, earthly life and exaltation respectively, then the problem arises: if *heauton ekenōsen* refers to the surrender of the servant's life, how is there balance when, within the first strophe, there is a jump from pre-existence to the death on the cross?[39] In his mature writing on this subject, Jeremias does not explicitly say that the three stages of Christ's existence correspond precisely with the division of three strophes.[40] He does explain that I, 1–2 and II, 1–2 are antitheses and I, 3–4, and II, 3–4, are synonymous parallels. Thus the three stages of Christ's existence are contained within the parallels in the first two strophes of the hymn.

Can we draw any conclusions from the evidence and discussions concerning the literary genre and the structure of the hymn? There is evidence of singing of hymns and psalms at worship in early NT times. These songs presumably included OT Psalms. There are strong indications that NT hymns celebrating Christ were also included, although we only possess them in written form. The Philippians hymn celebrates the central paschal mystery of Christ, his death and resurrection, in an early poetic form that deliberately draws upon a christological interpretation of the suffering servant of Deutero-Isaiah. It remains a possibility that this hymn was sung during the Eucharistic celebration, and its antiquity would suggest

37. Jeremias, *Central Message of New Testament*, 76.

38. R. Martin, *Early Christian Confession*, 8.

39. R. Martin, "Form-analysis," 619.

40. Jeremias, "*Zu Phil 2.7*," 187.

its origin in the Jerusalem Church. However, this latter conclusion depends upon whether the hymn was pre-Pauline.

PRE-PAULINE HYMN

Another question presents itself when one meets such a hymnic passage in the New Testament. Who wrote it? The general tendency is to regard the Philippians hymn as pre-Pauline.[41] This position is supported by the existence of several other apparently pre-Pauline hymns in his letters, and the ancient character of the language and theology of this hymn. Without entering the slippery ground of just what letters are authentically Pauline and, of these, to what extent they may admit of scribal or community redaction, it can be safely stated that the letter to the Philippians is generally considered as authentically Pauline, although composed in stages.

But whether the hymn was composed by Paul or was drawn by him from some other source admits of several suggestive possibilities. (1) Could it have been composed by Paul at an earlier date for some other Church or even for the Philippian Church and inserted in this letter? (2) Could it have been composed by a disciple of Paul?[42] (3) Could it have been composed by someone outside of Paul's influence and adopted by Paul? (4) Was it simply part of Paul's composition at the time of the letter writing? These are the questions that arise in the discussion of the origin of the hymn. The discussion centers around questions one and three.[43]

There is good evidence that Paul was capable of writing something poetic. Someone with his background in Judaism knew Old Testament poetry. Paul's hymn to *agapē* in 1 Cor 13 is the classic example of his power of literary and poetic inspiration. One could

41. Feuillet, "*l'Hymne christologique,*" 482.

42. Beare, *Commentary on Philippians*, 78.

43. Those who hold for Pauline authorship include: A. Deissmann, H. Lietzmann, W. D. Davies, E. Stauffer, L. Cerfaux, G. B. Caird, A. Feuillet, R. P. Martin, (*Early Christian Confession*, 16 and "Form-analysis of Philippians," 615).

quote several other passages containing a striking use of parallelism and rhetorical, if not lyrical, style that set them on the thin line between prose and poetry.[44]

There are four major reasons why authors do not consider this song to be written by Paul, and why it probably antedates the composition of the letter to the Philippians: (1) style, (2) context, (3) language, and (4) theology. Of these reasons, style offers the weakest argument against Pauline authorship, if one considers his Semitic background and his artistic gift for thinking and composing in parallels. On the other hand, scholars have pointed out the many liturgical sections that seem to be separate types of hymnal or creedal formula within the New Testament letters.[45] Yet it is more characteristic of Paul to change such a formula for his own purposes. This would explain the Pauline glosses, if such exist in the hymn.

The question of the context of the hymn overlaps with some questions about the language. It is generally agreed that the context of the Philippians hymn is of such a nature that the sudden presence of the profound hymnic parallels so shift the mood, sentiment, language, and thought that it comes as a "purple-patch,"[46] and so presses one to conclude, minimally, that the author did not compose this piece at the same time that he wrote his preceding exhortation. It might help in this regard to compare how other poetic pieces are related to their respective letters, e.g., 1 Cor 13; Col; Eph; etc.

Offsetting the sudden appearance of the hymn are the literary affinities between other sections of the letter and the hymn. There seems to be a certain unity of vocabulary and thematic elements between the hymn and other points Paul is making in the letter.

44. 1 Thess 5:14–22; Gal 5:16026; 1 Cor 1:18–21; Rom 8:31–39; 11:33–36; 16:25–27; 2 Cor 4:7–10; 6:3–10; 11:23–31; Col 1; Eph 1. Feuillet lists most of these in "*l'Hymne christologique*," 483.

45. Boismard, "*Liturgie Baptismale;*" *St. John's Prologue*; *Quatre Hymnes Baptismales*.

46. Hunter, *Paul and His Predecessors*, 42.

The relationship of similar language is based on the fact that such a relationship in vocabulary in given actions in other Pauline letters seems to illustrate a principle behind his letters. Paul uses similar vocabulary over definite series of related lines.[47]

Christ's *heauton ekenōsen*/"he emptied himself" is contrasted against community *kenodoxia*/"vainglory" (2:3), acting according to rivalry and vainglory, and "the looking of each one to his own interest" (2:4). Thus the antithesis with the "mind of Christ" is set up in terms of the community disunity. *Tapeinophrosyne*/"humility" (2:3) prepares for *etapeinōsen*/"he humbled himself," and *harpagmon hēgēsato*/"he did not consider clinging (to equality with God)," reinforces *hegoumenoi hyperechontes*/"deeming others better than themselves" (2:3). *Echaristhē*/"it was given" (1:29) prepares for *echarisato*; *eis doxan kai epainon Theou*/"to the glory and praise of God" (1:11) prepares for *eis doxan Patros*/"to the glory of God the Father" (2:11).

Vestiges of the hymnic vocabulary are also noticeable in subsequent passages of the letter. *Hēgēsthai*/"deemed" is taken up in 2:25; 3:7–8; *heurethō*/"discover" occurs in 3:9; *schēma* occurs in *metaschēmatisei* 3:21; *etapeinōsen*/"humbled" in *tapeinōseōs* in 3:21; 4:12; *morphē*/"form" in *symmorphon* 3:21, and *symmorphizomenos*/"conformed" 3:10. *Hypēkoos*/"obedient" is echoed in *hypēkousate* 2:12.[48]

However, if a case is to be made for the intrinsic relationship of the hymn with the rest of the letter, the thematic relations are stronger than the verbal affinities. The notable themes of this short letter, 1,539 words, seem to be joy, rejoicing (altogether eleven times, 1:3, 18, 25; 2:2, 17, 28, 29; 3:1; 4:1, 4, 10), humility which is associated with an attitude of mind regarding suffering and which corrects disunity, and finally the working of God in the Christian who works out his salvation, (2:12–18a). The unity and harmony

47. Feuillet, "*l'Hymne*," 496; e.g., Rom 7:7; 9:24–32; 10:12; 12:19; 1 Cor 1:18–20; 1:29–31; 2 Cor 3:15–16; 9:5.

48. Feuillet, "*l'Hymne christologique*," 495.

which result from the Christian attitude constitutes the immediate context for the hymn: "thinking the same things, having the same love, being one in soul, thinking one thing," (2:2). Zerwick suggests the main point of the hymn might be elicited by the use of the article which shows "Paul is thinking of some definite 'one thing' known to him and to the Philippians, filling the minds and hearts of all and effecting a unity of spirit; the article in *tē tapeinophrosynē* suggests that humility proper to Christians which Paul has so often inculcated and on which he is about to insist once more . . ."[49]

The joy and encouragement Paul gives to his Philippians over their fellowship for the spread of the good news (1:5) has a particular application for Euodia and Syntyche who were disagreeing (4:2–3). Chapters 1 and 3 suggest deeper sources of disunity (1:15–18, 27–30). This may be arising from those who were teaching contrary to Paul, that to become a Christian one had first to become a Jew, (3:2). Paul eloquently renews the mystery of his own vocation, so intimately connected with the mystery of the call of the Gentiles, a call to unity in Christ. Thus the Judaizers, against whom the great theme of justification by faith becomes so richly developed in Galatians and Romans, may here be the occasion for the call to unity, (3:9). This "party" conflict may be the same disturbance mentioned in 1 Cor 1.

In the immediate context of the hymn, the attitude toward unity and harmony is especially stressed, (2:1–5). This is a state of mind that is appreciated in struggle, opposition, and suffering, (1:27–30). There is a close analogy in expression and meaning between this attitude of unity, which demands a fellowship of spirit, and that total disposition of being "in the Spirit" that Paul develops more fully in Galatians and Romans. This positive attitude is seen in Christ in Phil 2. Its opposite kind of thinking, *sarkikos,* "fleshly" or "self-centered," is contrasted in Phil 3:16–21. The theme of unity which results from one's attitude of mind and which determines one's choices in life offer an argument against those who dispute

49. Zerwick, *Biblical Greek,* 54.

the unity of authorship in this letter. It is interesting to note how Paul introduces another major consideration of unity in Rom 12:16 with similar language.

Following the theme of martyrdom proposed by Lohmeyer, it has been suggested that the "he emptied himself" of 2:7 was the inspiration for Paul's writing "If I am poured out" 2:17, "and that the whole passage is really a vigorous expression of what had become for the Apostle, in his later years something of a magnificent obsession."[50] This interpretation may lean too heavily on the idea of Paul's last Roman captivity at the time of writing. It does respect the attitude of Paul who considered himself the *doulos tou Christou*/"the servant or slave of Christ," and who was experiencing suffering at the time of this letter writing, 1:29; 3:10. The affinities of language and themes between the hymn and the letter could be explained therefore, (1) because Paul wrote both, (2) Paul chose the hymn because it was appropriate to his thoughts at the time, (3) the hymn writer had heard Paul's preaching.

In order to decide upon the theme of the letter, which is influenced by Paul's state of life and attitude during this period, the date of the letter must be considered. The chronology of Paul's writing influences judgments about the development of his thought and the background for various teachings in each writing period.[51]

There are almost as many opinions about the dating of this letter as there are on the source and interpretation of the hymn. Three different periods are suggested for the authorship of the letter: Rome, AD 58–60, Ephesus ca. AD 56, and Caesarea AD 56–58. The third, though once popular, seems to be less seriously regarded today. That leaves Rome or Ephesus.

The arguments for later authorship during the Roman captivity are based on the reference to the *praetorium* guard in 1:13, and Caesar's household at 4:22, which seem to refer to circumstances of a Roman captivity. Also in favor of the Roman captivity is the

50. Furness, "Authorship of Philippians," 241, n. 7.

51. Stanley, "Pauline Soteriology."

mental and physical attitude and condition of Paul, which supposes he has been to Philippi more than once before, and is now nearing the end of his life. This late captivity context for composition has the weight of tradition.[52]

The reasons against the Roman period include the distance between Rome and Philippi for so many trips (four) and the exchange of information about Epaphroditus. The trip to Spain (Rom 15:28) would have occupied much of Paul's time if he ever made it. The reference to the Judaizers indicates the concern that occupied his mind during his writing period, contemporaneous with his third missionary journey. Perhaps the conflict of 1 Cor 1 is the more immediate background.

Therefore, an unmentioned Ephesian captivity is suggested on the strength of the early language, style, and thought of the letter, and on the fact that Paul suffered more imprisonments than are accounted for in Acts; see 2 Cor 1:8–9. This imprisonment could have occurred during the time of the riot at Ephesus, Acts 19:20 on the third missionary journey, AD 53–57. Ephesus seems to have been his base of operations during these years.

Furthermore, Paul has received no alms from Philippi since he was in Thessalonica on the second journey 4:16, because the Philippians had no opportunity of giving alms to him 4:10. But by the time Paul is imprisoned in Rome, he had twice visited the Philippians, Acts 20:2, 6, when he could have been given financial support.

The context of the hymn does not necessarily rule out Pauline authorship, and the discussion over the date of the letter adds more questions than answers to the problems. The convergence of the evidence seems to point strongly to the Ephesian captivity hypothesis. This would place the composition of the hymn at least before AD 57, presuming it is pre-Pauline. We now wish to discuss elements that argue against Paul's composition of the hymn, the language and the theology.

52. Wikenhauser, *New Testament Introduction*, 434 ff.

There are roughly four classes of language used in this hymn that, at least by the norm of occurrence elsewhere in the Bible, weigh against Pauline authorship: (1) those words that occur nowhere else in the NT; (2) those words or combinations that never occur elsewhere in Paul; (3) those grammatical expressions that are not standard Greek; (4) those words that are rare occurrences in Paul or are only used by him in a different way.

The words that are *hapax legomena* for Paul are *morphē*, and *morphē doulou, kenoun heauton, katachthōnios, en tō onomati Iēsou*. The words that occur nowhere else in the NT are *harpagmos*, and *hyperypsoun*. Concerning the latter, we know that Paul enjoys making up compound verbs to describe something unusual in the Christian life. The words and phrases that are not standard Greek expressions are *isa Theō, heuretheis hōs,* and *ekenoun heauton* 2:6, 7. Paul writes a Hellenized, Semitic-flavored Greek, so the presence of Semitic-like phrases alone does not cancel consideration of Pauline authorship. The words that are rare for Paul in this way are: *schēma* (1 Cor 7:31), *hypēkoos* (2 Cor 2:9) and *charizomai* which Paul never uses with reference to Christ. Some of this vocabulary is accounted for by the references to a Hebrew original of Deutero-Isaiah while other phrases suppose a Greek translation: 2:10 follows the LXX and 2:6–9 draw from the Hebrew of Is 53.

This striking collection of unusual vocabulary in one central christological hymn does not argue conclusively against Pauline authorship. There are many passages in his writings where he employs unusual vocabulary, presumably familiar to his readers, which he does not use again, (e.g., 2 Cor 3–4). This is partly his unique charismatic and creative contribution to Christianity. His christological vocabulary on the contrary, employs a rather consistent description of the redemptive action of Christ in his death and resurrection and the relation of this movement within the Father's initiative. The redemptive vocabulary of the hymn is more reminiscent of the early kerygmatic speeches in Acts. Thus the presence of unusual vocabulary and the absence of fuller Pauline language strongly suggest that Paul is borrowing from some source.

Closely related with this language problem is the theology standing behind it. What is strikingly absent is the redemptive interpretation of Christ's death in terms of the expiatory language, which states that it was done "for us" or "for many" or "for our sins." What is strange is to find a hymn which praises Christ's death and exaltation in the Deutero-Isaian language of the servant but which does not use the presumably related *hyper* or redemptive formula.[53] Some hold the hymn was not influenced by the servant of God theme.[54] Although the precise atonement formula is absent from the hymn, the context introduces the redemptive idea by exhorting the Christians to live for others: "Let each of you look not only to his own interests, but also to the interest of others" (2:4). This Pauline introduction to the hymn may indicate that he is using a source which lacked this interpretation, and which he faithfully records without changing it. Paul introduces and concludes it with practical formulations of the significance of the living actions of Christ for his Philippian community.

It is also suggested that Paul may have avoided more frequent and elaborate use of the servant theology because Christ's "resurrection was conceived by Paul not so much as a vindication of His death or as a reward for His transcendent obedience—a view suggested by the servant theology—but rather 'for our justification.'"[55] Paul also transforms or develops a key aspect of the servant theme by applying to his own ministry the meaning and understanding of *doulos*. Paul calls himself a "slave" in relation to Christ his master, but calls his service to the Gospel, *diakonia* or "ministry," to emphasize a relationship to the work to be done or the cause to be served.[56] Likewise absent is the customary Pauline resurrection

53. Ibid., 95–96.

54. Feuillet, "*l'Hymne christologique*," 357.

55. Stanley, *Apostolic Church in New Testament*, 346.

56. Ibid., 312–51.

vocabulary: *anistēmi*/"rise again" (eight times) and *egeiro*/"rise up" (forty times). In its place is the expression "to be very much lifted up," *hyperypsoun*, which is used without the prefix four times by John (3:14; 8:28; 12:32, 34) and twice by Peter in Acts (2:33; 5:31). Both the Hebrew *nasah* and the Aramaic *zegap* , which lies behind this expression, contain two dimensions: "to crucify," or "hang" and "to raise up."[57] This is probably a more ancient formula explaining the crucifixion and resurrection mystery.[58] The hymn adds *hyper* which sounds more like the Hebrew *meʾod*/"lifted very high" of Is 52:13.

There is a similarity between the theology of the hymn with Peter's speeches in Acts. This similarity lies in the common expressions of *hypsoun*, the designation of Christ as *pais*, (four times), and the reference to the name Jesus (14 times) in Acts.

The customary Pauline ecclesial dimension, which is characteristic of the hymnic structured sections of Colossians and Ephesians, seems to be noticeably absent from this hymn. The references to confession and homage imply ecclesial worship, and the descriptive roles of Christ as servant, son of man, new Adam may contain implicitly the notion of a corporate personality. Yet Paul is usually more explicit when he relates Christ's paschal mystery with the Christian mystery, the church. The concentrated build up towards the hymn in terms of correct Christian thinking, *phronein*, which is common in Pauline vocabulary, (five times in Philippians, six times in other letters), gives one the impression that Paul is respecting a separate confessional formulation of Christ's attitude and decision toward life. Finally, the Son of man as pre-existent seems to be part of the pre-Pauline Christian tradition.[59]

On the other hand, several themes characteristic of Pauline theology are apparent in the hymn. The most important of these is the Adam-Christ correlation which many consider an original

57. R. Brown, *Gospel According to John*, 146.

58. Black, "Son of Man Problem," 315–16.

59. Hunter, *Paul and His Predecessors*, 86–87.

conception for Paul.[60] The earlier dating of the letter may also be supported by presence of this same theme in 1 Cor 15:21–22 and Rom 5:12–21. One of the indications of the "new Adam" Christology is contained in the word *morphē*, a word practically synonymous with *eikōn* in the LXX. The LXX also uses *eikōn* and *doxa* in parallel fashion, (Job 4:16). "The form of God," that Christ did not cling to was the "divine glory," as John puts it, "the glory which I had with thee before the world was," according to John Calvin.[61] There are echoes of the "likeness" language, *morphē, heuretheis hōs, homoiōmati*, in the *bi demuth* of Gen 5:1, 3; in the *kebar* of Dan 7:13; the *kidemuth* of Dan 10:16; the *kemar*ʾ*eh* of Dan 8, 15; 10:18.[62] However this "likeness" language also belongs to the son of man tradition and there is equally strong evidence of its influence in the hymn.

> We can now argue that the earlier words about "being made in the likeness of men" (*en homoiōmati anthrōpōn genomenos*) is even closer to the text of Daniel, since the variant (*en homoiōmati anthrōpou genomenos*) "being made in the likeness of man," has now the support of P46; and *en homoiōmati anthrōpou* is the Danielic *kebarnash*, "one like a man." At Rev 14:14 the expression appears in an unmistakable allusion to Dan 7:13 as *homoion huion* (*huiō* v. 1) *anthrōpou*.[63]

If we insist that Paul originated the Adam-Christ typology in his evangelization, and if we insist that such imagery is present in the language of the hymn, then we must assume that the hymn comes from Pauline, not pre-Pauline composition. But the Son of Man tradition arises from the teaching of the historical Jesus, obviously older than that which preached Christ as the "New Adam."

When Paul develops his threefold image theology: Christ is the image of God; man is the image of God; the Christian is the im-

60. Feuillet, "*l'Hymne christologique*," 490.
61. R. Martin, *Early Christian Confession*, 18.
62. Feuillet, "*l'Hymne christologique*," 371.
63. Black, "Son of Man Problem," 315.

age of Christ, he uses the *eikōn*/"image" of the LXX Gen 1:26–27; 5:1, 3; 9:6. That he considers this related to the *doxa*/"glory," can be seen in 2 Cor 3:18 and 4:4–6. Feuillet relates the language of this passage in 2 Cor to Christ as the Wisdom of God.[64] Reference to the "obedience" of Christ is also part of the new Adam theme. In Rom 5:12–21 Christ's obedience is contrasted with the disobedience of Adam. Even Paul's use of *de* has been considered part of his expression when mentioning the scandal of the Cross, 1 Cor 15:56–57.

What can be said from this evidence concerning the question of the pre-Pauline authorship of the hymn? The poetic features of its structure and the additional weight of the peculiar vocabulary incline one toward a pre-Pauline source. The use of similar vocabulary in other passages within the letter may be explained by the central inspirational role that the hymn played in Paul's composition and communication. To claim some verses in the hymn are expressions of the Adam-Christ typology and still claim the hymn is pre-Pauline, does not take anything away from Paul's later development of this analogy in 1 Cor 15 and Rom 5.

EXEGESIS

2:5 *Touto phroneite en hymin ho kai en Christō Iēsou*/Think this way among yourselves which also is in Christ Jesus . . .

Touto is seldom used to point to a following clause (e.g., Luke 5:31); it is somewhat more frequently used as preparation for a subordinate clause with *hoti, hina* or for an infinitive or substantive.[65] The use of *touto* as anticipatory is less strange if we consider the emphatic use of *kai* following the relative as in Rom 16:7; 1 Cor 1:6–8; Phil 4:10, where *kai* accentuates the fact that the relative clause is in balance with the preceding clause; it is complementary or correlative with it. The emphasis is usually brought out by implicitly comparing the word that follows the emphatic *kai,* with

64. Feuillet, "*l'Hymne christologique,*" 492.

65. Blass, *Greek Grammar of New Testament*, 151.

another similar word (noun or verb), in the clause which preceded or follows: e.g., Col 2:11–12; Eph 1:11. Thus the unusual use of *touto* can be explained grammatically to answer a question from Lohmeyer.[66] It also functions as a bridge, introducing the line that serves as a transition from that attitude which should be in the community to that attitude which was in Christ.

We have already mentioned the use of *phroneite*, its function as an imperative, and its common use in Paul. However the interpretation of the second half of the line depends on the use of *kai* after the relative and whether the "in Christ Jesus" repeats the *en hymin* or adds another element which then needs its own verb to be supplied. Feuillet adds "was" to complete the phrase.

The resolution of the problem as to just what the phrase "which also was/is in Christ Jesus" means, is conditional on whether the hymn was used by Paul as merely a paraenesis or moral exhortation, or as revealing the soteriological attitude of Christ. If we translate "have those sentiments toward one another which are yours being members 'in Christ Jesus,'" a transition is still needed to arrive at the thinking of Christ. One is persuaded toward this meaning by the frequent use of the customary Pauline baptismal formula "in Christ Jesus." However, "in Christ Jesus" seems to refer ahead to the coming confession of the event of the historical Jesus rather than backwards to the ecclesial Christ in the Philippian community. This would seem to be confirmed if the hymn is taken as the celebration of Christ's saving acts. It would also seem to follow from the immediately preceding context. Thus the better version would be, "Have that attitude among yourselves which was the attitude of Christ Jesus."

2:6 *Hos en morphē Theou hyparchōn, ouch harpagmon hēgēsato to einai isa Theō*/who subsisting in the form of God did not consider equality with God something to be grasped . . .

This line opens the hymn proper and exposes the exegete to a flood of opinions on every word. The whole phrase to 7a depends

66. Lohmeyer, *Kyrios Jesus*.

on the relative pronoun *hos*, and consequently refers to the same subject, the person of Christ. *En morphē Theou hyparchōn* begins the problems of exegesis. Does this refer to Christ's divine pre-existence? Can *morphē* be taken in the sense of *ousia* as a nature predicate?[67] Does it refer to his earthly existence and the divine qualities he manifested and claimed? Or is it merely an external descriptive term? Lightfoot in his contrast between *morphē* and *schēma* took *morphē* "in a sense substantially the same which it bears in Greek philosophy."[68] Most authors today look to a Hebraic background to explain this word. They find it more closely related to the "image and likeness" language that is predicated of Christ in the fullest sense.[69] *Hyparchōn* adds to *hos* or *genomenos* a note of continuance, of "being originally"[70] or "fundamental possession" as 1 Cor 11:7. Martin thinks the whole phrase strongly echoes the Johannine "the glory which I had with thee before the world was" John 17:5.[71] *Morphē* stands for the inner reality expressed in outward appearance. Jeremias suggests it intends to render the Heb. *toʾaro*/"appearance" of Is 52:14; 53:2. Scholars say *toʾaro* means more than simple appearance in English. It is like derivatives from the Latin, *gero*, meaning the way one conducts oneself, the way he manifests himself by his actions in the world. The *morphē*/*toʾaro* similarity connects this verse with the other servant motifs in other sections of the hymn. It is not absolutely clear that it refers to Christ's pre-existence. John's prologue and the hymn to Christ in Colossians are much more definite regarding pre-existence. However it does indicate a fundamental ground of being against which the historical decisions and actions of Jesus create a striking contrast.

67. Lightfoot, *Epistle to Philippians*, 127–33.

68. Ibid., 132.

69. Feuillet, "*l'Hymne christologique*," 371 ff.

70. Prat, *Theology of St. Paul*, 315–16.

71. R. Martin, *Early Christian Confession*, 18.

The next phrase has a long and tragic exegetical and theological history from Arianism to the present day.[72] The extra-biblical Greek, active meaning of *harpagmos* as the act of robbery or usurpation, is now largely abandoned.[73] The passive meaning which the Greek Fathers understood as equivalent to *harpagma* in the NT, could mean "clung to," *res rapta*, or "to be clung to," something to be possessed in the future, *res rapienda*.[74] A third possibility could be the classical meaning of a "piece of good fortune," which interpretation creeps into Aquila's text of Is 53:12.[75] Some even stretch this puzzling expression to a relation with the apocalyptic violence connected with the coming of the kingdom in Matt 11:12.[76]

One way out of this tangle is to focus on the *to einai isa Theō* which is in apposition to the *harpagmon*. This phrase has its own difficulties, using the plural neuter adjective *isa* as an adverb.[77] "To be equal with God" means to be on the same rank as God. "This unusual wording suggests that Paul has also in view the instance and example of another person who *did* count equality with God as a desirable thing, and from a favored position *did* aspire to his own glory."[78] In other words, the best explanation, perhaps the only explanation of this line, exists in the "Pauline" contrast of the two Adams.[79] The temptation of the serpent was, "you will be like God" (Gen 3:5). God speaks ironically about this after the Fall, "Behold, the man has become like one of us" (Gen 3:22). This temptation is repeated elsewhere in the OT. "I will make myself like the Most

72. Henry, "*Kénose*," 23 ff.
73. R. Martin, *Early Christian Confession*, 19.
74. Prat, *Theology of St. Paul*, 318–19; 461–62.
75. R. Martin, *Early Christian Confession*, 21 n. 22; 50–51.
76. Griffiths, "*Harpagmos* and *Heauton ekenōsen*," 237-39.
77. Blass, *Greek Grammar of New Testament*, 205–6.
78. R. Martin, *Early Christian Confession*, 22.
79. Cullman, *Christology of the New Testament*, 177.

High," (Is 14:12 ff.). The rebellion and fall of Satan in Enoch 29:4–5 may also be related to this expression.[80]

Thus "to be like God" expresses the biblical notion of sin, which is related to the Pauline meaning of "covet" in Rom 7:7. The idea of coveting in LXX Greek never had sexual connotation, but was the primary desire that was behind all sin, "to want to be like God."[81] If this phrase refers to Christ's refusal to covet a manner of life contrary to his father's will, it should be related to other expressions of the sinlessness of Christ, and to the temptations of Christ. A similar NT expression allies this resistance of temptation with the acceptance of the Cross: "Looking to Jesus the pioneer and perfector of our faith, who for the joy that was set before him endured the cross, despising the shame, and is seated at the right hand of the throne of God" (Heb 12:2). Christ rejected the original sin of humanity, "the desire to be like God."

The phrase "He did not consider equality with God something to be possessed" does not refer to a discarding of "being in the form of God" but rather to the earthly existence of Christ who chose a human life of suffering weakness and death in contrast to the choice of Adam. This interpretation influences the meaning of "being in the form of God" making it a reference to Christ's earthly existence, since it was only a being of this proportion and power who could reverse the primal grasping of the man who desired "to be like God."[82]

2:7 *Alla heauton ekenōsen, morphēn doulou labōn, en homoiōmati anthrōpōn genomenos kai schēmati heuretheis hōs anthrōpos*/but he emptied himself, taking the form of a servant, becoming like other humans, and in appearance found as a human . . .

Alla sets up the antithesis to the preceding *ouch harpagmon* etc., and should be translated "but." The phrase *heauton ekenōsen*/"he emptied himself" has been demonstrated

80. R. Martin, *Early Christian Confession*, 53–54.

81. Lyonnet, *Exegesis Epistulae ad Romanos*, 72–83.

82. Feuillet, "*l'Hymne christologique*," 367.

by Jeremias to be a translation of the Hebrew of Is 53:12, *erah . . . napsho*/"he surrendered his life." This interpretation deals a strong blow to kenotic theories. It does not look back to the emptying of divine form or qualities except as a resistance to the human desire to be like God. Rather it looks ahead to the positive action of Christ's death, the central redemptive decision for sacrifice, the surrender of life on the Cross. The LXX translation of Is 53:12 with *paredothē* shows the tendency to attribute the active initiative of salvation to Yahweh and make the servant's role one of spontaneously offering himself.[83]

Some authors observe that a special grammatical relationship is involved in the three aorist participles *labōn*, *genomenos*, and *heuretheis*, following the aorist indicative, *ekenōsen*.[84] Generally in the NT, the aorist participle, which connotes more the aspect of action than time, when accompanied with an aorist indicative, expresses an action that is secondary but anterior in relation to the principle action. If this is true, "Taking the form of a servant . . ." precedes the pouring out of his life, if not temporally, at least in order of priority of significance.[85]

If *heauton ekenōsen* is an action posterior to "taking the form of a slave or servant, becoming in the likeness of man, and found in appearance like a man," and if "he emptied himself" refers to the life-surrender of the Cross in the language of the suffering servant, then the structure of the hymn does not seem to follow a pattern of pre-existence, incarnation, death and exaltation. However, if the pattern of the hymn is basically one of chiastic and antithetic parallels, then one would not expect a neat one, two, three movement recalling the steps of the early kerygma. The difficulty of distinguishing stages of Christ's life is characteristic of Paul's focus of attention on the death-resurrection mystery of Christ climaxed in the glory of the Father. Paul does not distinguish a moment of

83. Feuillet, "*l'Hymne christologique*," 360.

84. Ibid., 362.

85. Moule, *Idiom-Book of NT Greek*, 100.

Incarnation separate from Christ's death. At most he expresses various "stages" of Christ's life in terms of level of existence; e.g., 2 Cor 8:9; Gal 4:4–5; Rom 8:3; also Heb 2:14–16; 10:5.[86]

That *heauton ekenōsen* points to Christ's death in terms of the suffering servant of Deutero-Isaiah is further confirmed by the expression "taking the form of a slave." *Doulos* is a familiar Pauline contrast with *Kyrios*; the slave-master relationship was well known in Hellenistic society. *Morphēn* has already been seen in relation to the *toʾaro* of Isaiah. Some wonder why *pais*/"youth" or "child" is not used, if the hymn is inspired by the same early strand of servant Christology that influenced Acts 3:13; 4:27, 30. Although the LXX does use *douleuein* in Is 53:11, according to Jeremias, it generally renders *ebed*/"servant" with *pais* rather than *doulos*. One explanation is that there may not be much distinction between the words as Aquila's version of Is 52:13 and 53:2 indicates. Another explanation concerns the development of understanding of the servant's death after his exaltation as Lord. The Christian who by the Spirit can address God as Abba, Father, is for Paul a *doulos* rather than a *pais*. Finally, *doulos* is a closer rendering of *ebed*.

The *RSV* translates *en homoiōmati anthrōpōn genomenos*, "being born in the likeness of men." *Homoiōmati* is the second likeness word designating the quality of appearance of this person. This vocabulary group strongly recalls the creation of man in the image and likeness of God in Gen 1:26, etc. This expression also suggests the one like the son of man in Daniel, whether one accepts the reading *anthrōpou* or *anthrōpōn*. "At Rev 14:14 the expression appears in an unmistakable allusion to Dan 7:13 as *homoion huion (huiō* v.1) *anthrōpou*."[87] This returns us to the question of pre-existence since the son of man of Daniel strongly suggests pre-existence. Moreover he is a transcendent figure, much above the abasement of the servant. This tension strikes the heart of the Christian paradox and reveals something about the mystery

86. R. Martin, *Early Christian Confession*, 25.

87. Black, "Son of Man Problem," 315.

of the union of these OT figures in Jesus. Finally, if the *k^{e}bar^{ʾe}nash* of Dan 7:13 stands behind the *anthrōpōn* of Phil 2:7, Black thinks it would be better to translate *genomenos* as "becoming" rather than to designate the historical point of birth.[88]

The last in the series of three participial expressions also recalls the language of Daniel describing the son of man, "and found in appearance like a man."[89] *Kai* corresponds with *alla* and intensifies it. *Schēma* refers more to one's outward manner of bearing. *Heuretheis* describes the situation similar to that in which the servant is found in Is 53:9; the LXX uses the same verb. Finally, *hōs anthrōpos*, an awkward Greek expression, is close to the Aramaic *k^{e}bar^{ʾe}nash* of Dan 7:13.[90]

2:8 *etapeinōsen heauton genomenos hypēkoos mechri thanatou, thanatou de staurou*/he humbled himself, becoming obedient even to death, death on the cross.

"He humbled himself" seems to repeat the thought of "he emptied himself." Feuillet thinks that the foregoing has been so obscure for the Gentile Christian convert, that Paul judges he should clarify it with his own expression; so he adds v. 8.[91] Although the verb "humble" is common in Paul's vocabulary, it also occurs in the LXX for Is 53:9 and has other OT parallels which describe the attitude of those who serve Yahweh, (Is 58:3). If this is a Pauline gloss to an older hymn, it may be introduced for the paraenetic purpose of relating this hymn to Christ to the Philippian community.

"Becoming obedient" stands out as a New Adam theme with Paul in Rom 5:19. It has echoes in the LXX rendering of Is 53:7. The obedience of Christ who does the will of his Father who sent him is a strong Johannine motif; John 8:29; 4:34; 5:30; 6:38. When the author of Hebrews writes: "He learned obedience through the things which he suffered," Heb 5:8, he refers to the

88. Ibid., 315.

89. Feuillet, "*l'Hymne christologique*," 377.

90. Blass, *Greek Grammar of New Testament*, 232.

91. Feuillet, "*l'Hymne christologique*," 494.

same christological attitude. *Hypakouē* is often used in the LXX translation of the OT to render *anawah*, the Hebrew word for "poverty."[92] What is most important about the new Adam and new creation that occurs in Christ is not that he dies, but that he is obedient to the Father. "Even to death" describes the extent to which Christ's love and obedience to the Father reaches. "Lohmeyer has pointed out how in Jewish theology, death is shown as a monarch, or even as a kingdom itself."[93] It is as a journey to a foreign kingdom as some interpret the meaning of Christ's descent into Hell in 2 Pet 3:18–22.

Since Lohmeyer, "death on a cross" has been considered by many as a Pauline gloss to an otherwise metrically balanced structure. "It would have special meaning for the Philippian readers [hearers] who [as Roman citizens] were residents in a Roman city where revulsion against this form of capital punishment would be very strong."[94] Death by crucifixion is the great *skandalon* for Paul, 1 Cor 1; Gal 3:13; 5:11; Rom 15:3. *De* has a progressive explanatory force.[95] Feuillet considers this use of *de* a Paulinism (1965, 493).

2:9 *Dio kai ho Theos auton hyperypsōsen kai echarisato autō to onoma to hyper pan onoma*/Therefore God greatly exalted him and bestowed on him the name above every name . . .

The common expression *dio kai*[96] introduces the shift to the second part of the hymn, which employs a different style and notably changes the mood and tone as well as the meaning of the hymn. Now the Father, *ho Theos*, mentioned with the characteristic article, takes the initiative. "Therefore" sets off this transition. Stanley understands it as an expression of early "merit" theology.[97] But, if it echoes the exaltation of the servant in Is 53:12, it may be

92. Ahern, "Introduction," 8.

93. R. Martin, *Early Christian Confession*, 31.

94. Ibid.

95. Zerwick, *Biblical Greek*, 157.

96. Ibid., 155.

97. Stanley, *Apostolic Church in New Testament*, 101.

interpreted as the announcement and transition vocabulary introducing a salvation oracle. The first half of the hymn describes the vocation and call of Jesus who freely worked out his mission in our world; the second half describes the fulfillment of that vocation. The correlative to the freely chosen obedience, which goes as far as self-emptying, is not so much a reward as the completion of the Father's mission.

"More than exalted him" employs a verb that seems to be a very early expression of the exaltation of the son of man, Acts 2:33; 5:31; John 3:14; 8:32, 34. John's usage corresponds with the Philippians passage better than the description in Acts.[98] It is based, as we noted above, on an Aramaic verb that can mean both "hang" as in crucifixion, and "be lifted up." One who "emptied himself" so low as to suffer and die obedient to the Father is "super-exalted." The *hyper* seems to be rendering of the Heb. adverb, *m*ᵉʾ*od*, "very much" of Is 52:13. In the LXX the same verb is used with "glorified" to intensify by synonymous parallelism the notion of the raising of the servant very high. This unusual use of *hyper* to make a compound verb occurs in another significant passage, Rom 5:20, to show how Christ's obedience was for us a favor far abounding the disobedience of Adam.

The use of *echarisato*, "God gave him the name as a pure favor," is "unparalleled in the Pauline writings."[99] It richly prepares for the gift signified by the name. The divine gift is in contrast with the refusal of Christ's self-aggrandizement in 2:6. The name that is granted which is above every name is *Kyrios*, the definitive contrast to *doulos*; the role of the human Jesus as poor, suffering, obedient, humble, servant is contrasted with the divine gift of Lordship, power, rule and authority.

2:10 *Hina en tō onomati Iēsou pan gony kampsē epouraniōn kai epigeiōn kai katachthoniōn*/that in the name of Jesus every knee should bend in heaven, on earth, and under the earth . . .

98. Black, *Aramaic Approach to Gospels*, 315.

99. Stanley, *Apostolic Church in New Testament*, 348.

The development of the meaning of "the name" employs the enthronement language of homage to Yahweh, "To me every knee shall bow, every tongue shall swear," Is 45:23. It comes from Isaiah's confession in the universal salvific power of the one God and his utter fidelity to his word, Is 45:22 ff. Paul uses the expression in the context of the universal Lordship of Christ in Rom 14:11 "As I live, says the Lord, every knee shall bow to me, and every tongue shall give praise to God." In the homage of the East there is no distinction between bowing the knee and full prostration.[100]

Names in the OT were of the utmost importance.[101] The NT develops this theology of the name of Yahweh along with the name of Jesus. There seems to be an ambiguity as to whether the name of Jesus is meant as the object of this homage, or whether it refers to the name "Lord," which the historical Jesus receives by his resurrection and exaltation. In Acts, the Apostles appeal to the name of Jesus Christ to heal, 3:6, to save, 4:12, to preach, 5:40 and 8:12, and to suffer, 5:42. It is Paul who preaches in the name of the Lord, Acts 9:15, 28. Just as there develops a certain tension in the first part of the hymn between the roles of Jesus Christ as the son of man and as the suffering servant, so in the theology of his new relationship with the power and glory of the Father, there is a certain tension evident between his historical name Jesus, his Messianic title, Christ, and his exalted royal title, Lord. It is not so much an exegetical problem as the result of a mystery that this human historical temporal Jesus who fulfills major OT prophecies is not only actively present with humans, but is present with God as Lord. "The name" in the Hebrew mentality stands for the Person—the ultimate reality behind the title. How great is this Lordship is emphasized by the homage of the three levels of the known cosmos which symbolizes the whole universe, the living and the dead, all heavenly and earthly beings, Jews and Gentiles, the entire church, all humanity, the entire universe. Witness to the Lord is cosmic.

100. Schlier, "*Gonu*," 738.

101. McKenzie, *Dictionary of the Bible*, 603–5.

The appeal to the expanse of the known universe as witness and participant in the worship of Jesus as Lord in this passage is a reversal of the way idolatry is portrayed in the most important confession of the OT, the confession of the one, true God. Each time the Ten Commandments are presented in the OT, they contain the prohibition of the worship of idols made from anything in heaven, on earth, or under the earth; Exod 20:4–5; Deut 5:8–9. Jesus represents our created humanity. His humanity is created. The one created reality out of the entire universe we may fully worship is Jesus as Lord.

2:11 *kai pasa glōssa exomologēsetai hoti Kyrios Iēsous Christos eis doxan Theou Patros*/and every tongue profess that Jesus Christ is Lord to the glory of God the Father.

The final verse fills out the human acts of homage recognizing the Lordship of Jesus whose resurrection confirms him in this absolute relation to the Father. *Exomologēsetai*, the aorist subjunctive is preferred to the future indicative reading which occurs in most MSS. *Homologia* seems to be an introductory confessional formula for the early church. It is related to the *Shema* of the Jewish synagogue. "From its use in the daily recitations, in the temple and in the synagogue, the *Shema* may properly be called a confession acclamation, or acknowledgment of the faith of Judaism, as distinct from prayer offered to God."[102] Jesus used this formal confession and later the Apostles use it of Jesus.

> The opening phrases of the *Shema* are recited by Jesus Mk 12:29, *eis ho Theos* and *monos Theos* are expressed and other larger statements suggest the importance of the confession and its formulary expression for both Christian and Jew.[103]

A *homologia* in the early church would include: (1) a naming of Jesus, a title, and (2) a reference to his basic personal relationship and to his work. Thus we have in the hymn a fundamental early Christian formula. Perhaps we have here Eucharistic overtones if

102. Neufeld, *Earliest Christian Confession*, 36.

103. Ibid., 37.

we can show that "the LXX verb for thanksgiving is *exomologesthai*; but this verb is increasingly replaced in Christian usage by the newer and more Hellenistic term *eucharistein*, so that the formula ultimately produces the name of the Eucharist."[104]

The marks of this passage reveal that: (1) Jesus is Lord, 1 Cor 12:3; 2 Cor 4:5; Rom 10:9; 2 Cor 1:20; (2) Jesus' Lordship is universal, Rom 14:8–9; (3) His Lordship is confessed, Rom 10:8–13, 16; and (4) his Lordship is ordered to the glory of the Father, 1 Cor 3:23; 11:3; 15:24, 28; 2 Cor 1:20; Rom 15:1–13; 16:27; Eph 1:6, 12, 14. The relation of Jesus to the glory of the Father is often overlooked in the discussions of the Christology of the hymn. However it is very characteristic of Paul to explicitly make this relationship, even in his most concentrated christological passages: 1 Cor 3:23; 1 Cor 11:3; 1 Cor 15:24, 28; Rom 15:1–13; 16:27. Finally, concerning the title Lord, it does not seem possible to affirm with assurance the course of development of the use of this title as a substitution for Yahweh in the LXX. It occurs frequently in the Psalms and Isaiah as a solemn title more than in the rest of the OT.

THEOLOGY

In the light of this survey of research, we shall try to form some judgment about what the hymn reveals about God, about Christ, and about the Christian faith. Until now we have concentrated our attention on reconstructing the process and possible ways the hymn entered Paul's letter to the Philippian community. Now we shall try to draw some of this information together and relate its meaning to present and future Christian communities. Again Paul guides us when he says that Scripture "was written for your sake," Rom 4:23; 15:4; 1 Cor 9:10. Since this is a task for biblical theology, it is instructive to consider some guidelines for that specific craft of theology.

Once one has determined the meaning of individual words from linguistic, semantic and philological viewpoints, it is neces-

104. J. Robinson, "Historicality of Biblical Language," 132–33.

sary to relate them to the higher viewpoints of their word combinations in phrases or sentences. Many word-groups constitute a formula carrying a special theological significance; e.g., "in Christ." Barr insists "The real bearer of the theological statement is the large complex, like the sentence."[105] "The sentence, unlike the word, is unique and non-recurrent."[106] Too much concentration on the theological concept in a single word may cause one to overlook how the sentence may relate distinct, different and new qualities to a frequently repeated word. Barr critiques the flood of new biblical dictionary use.

> The attempt in much recent biblical theology to demonstrate the existence of a biblical lexical stock of words or "concepts" (in this case what we may call "word-concepts" and "sentence-concepts") which are semantically distinctive, that is to say, which have a semantic distinctiveness which can be set in close correlation with the distinctiveness of the faith and theology of the Bible, is in principle a failure.[107]

Thus to understand the full meaning of what is revealed in this passage, it will pay to attend to the entire context of the hymn in Phil 2:1–18.

Biblical theology consists in the perception of the relationship between words, sentences, and concepts that cut across the various writings of the Bible, accompanied by attempts to discover patterns and themes that the authors are conveying. These patterns will have the variations of the *Sitz im Leben*, viewpoints, and intentions of distinct authors. This method of reading Scripture in the light of its inner relationships and development is built upon the critical approaches of historical, literary, and exegetical study. Having discovered and tested the validity of these relationships, if they are solid, they will support the weight of further theological formulations. They are open to the development of dogma. The

105. Barr, *Semantics of Biblical Language*, 265.

106. Ibid., 269.

107. Ibid., 269 ff.

dogma, in turn, must be continually corrected in the light of its historical formulation and dependence upon the insights of the contemporary culture in which it develops. Schillebeeckx writes,

> A dogma is the correct, though never exhaustive, hearing of a reality of revelation or of a word of revelation. And this is what gives rise to the immense difference between the development of faith and theological development.[108]

While the dogma must be continually open to its roots in revelation, the danger that it must always avoid is *eis-egesis*, reading something into Scripture. This sometimes occurs in the search for "proof-texts."[109] If the NT writers seem to have done this themselves, it was under the guidance and inspiration of the Spirit directing the faith of the church to incite fuller understanding of the revelation of God in Christ. It is called Midrash in the Rabbinic tradition. Schillebeeckx writes,

> The exegete tries to establish how the word of God was pronounced to the Jewish people and the early Church, and how it was heard by them. The dogmatic theologian, on the contrary, tries to ascertain how the selfsame word, already heard by Israel and the apostolic Church and yet directed to us in the twentieth century, may be heard by us without distortion.[110]

The entire NT gives us an example of this kind of work in the use of the OT. A continual searching of Scripture in faith is

108. Schillebeeckx, "Development of Dogma," 124–25.

109. "After the second session of Vatican Council II, Oscar Cullmann, studying the place of the Bible in the Council, noted that if several of the schemata had been nourished on an authentic biblical source, there were others which, in spite of many citations from the sacred books, had only a somewhat distant relationship with biblical thought: 'when we look more closely we note,' he says, 'that very often the numerous biblical references added in parenthesis are not the real basis of the exposition, but that they are only *dicta probantia* destined to establish, as an afterthought, a somewhat external relation between the already established text of the schema and the Bible.'" Cullmann, "*Bible et Concile*," 291, taken from Bosc, "Calvin to Present-Day Catholics," 29. Also Levie, "Critical Exegesis," 273–97.

110. Schillebeeckx, "Development of Dogma," 125.

both indicated and advised with an inspired sense of Midrash. The writings of Paul and John, of Luke and Matthew clearly reveal this searching of Scripture with the penetration of faith, to understand the meaning of the events and message of Jesus for the church. The NT writers had the guarantee of the church's inspiration and were apostolic vehicles of the constitutive revelation which was not yet closed. What they did, the dogmatic theologian tries to do for his/her day, in a purely scientific and therefore fallible way by means of scientific tools and human analogies.[111]

What can be said about the theology of the Philippian hymn? Historically it has played an important role in christological development, especially in the statements about the person and nature of Christ in the councils of Nicaea and Chalcedon. The Fathers and ecclesiastical writers regarded the opening lines as applying to the pre-existent Christ. In general they understood the "stripping" or "self-emptying" as referring to the Incarnation. What was stripped was the external glory and honor due to God. They understood "the form of God" as Christ's divinity, which they variously interpreted as *ousia, physis, theotēs* or *eikōn*. "The form of a slave" referred to his full humanness.[112]

Modern interpretation has thrown light on the titles of Christ, which appear elsewhere in Acts and the Gospels and in the doxologies of NT epistles. Concentrated study has been directed to the titles Lord, The Servant of God, The Son of Man, and the Second Adam.

The Lordship of Jesus is the early Christian confession in the resurrection and power of Jesus and the hope in his second coming. It is retained in one form in the Aramaic phrase *Maranatha*, "Lord, Come!" 1 Cor 16:22; it is expressed in Greek in several ways, e.g., "Come Lord Jesus!" Rev 22:20; 1 Cor 11:26. Sometimes Paul applies OT texts to Christ, but there is not a regular or nec-

111. Ibid., 132.

112. Prat, *Theology of St. Paul*, 456–65.

essary substitution of the Christian *Kyrios* for the OT *Adonai*.[113] Paul develops the use of Ps. 110 which the Lord himself used, and which the community used after the resurrection, especially in the speeches of Acts. The use of the title Lord is notably related to the Father in several places, 1 Cor 3:23; 11:3; 15:24, 28.

Is "the name above every name" Jesus or Lord, or does it refer to the divine basis for Lordship, which is an inaccessible, unspeakable reality, so much above every name, because it corresponds to the mysterious character of the ineffable tetragram?[114] In Acts it is the name Jesus Christ which is the source of power, although Paul refers to him as Lord. The NT writers did not think in the later theological-philosophical terms of person and nature. Moreover, they never identify Jesus with God the Father, *ho Theos*. But they do apply to Jesus OT formulas which belong to Yahweh.[115] In "the name" is some specific power, with a personal meaning which designates the role, office, function, ultimately the deepest reality of the bearer. As in the OT where the giving of a name was important, Abraham and Israel for example, so both the giving of the name and the taking of a new name is highly significant for the function of NT personalities. The change from Simon to Peter is in some analogous sense parallel in function to the new name "Lord" given to the risen Jesus. So, too, Saul of Tarsus becomes Paul the Apostle to the Gentiles. Thus the name bestowed on Jesus, "the name above every name," the one to which all creation bows and that all people confess is the name signifying God's powerful intervention in the history and nature of humanity by extending himself personally into time and space. But inasmuch as this name is predicated of a transcendent being it only inadequately, in the limited language of the liturgy, touches the ineffable mystery of the mission and of the divine Person behind the name.

113. Cerfaux, *Christ in St. Paul*, 469–72.

114. Ibid., 479.

115. McKenzie, *Dictionary of the Bible*, 605.

Finally, the title "Lord" grows out of the powerful resurrection mystery. For Paul, "Lord" designated the risen Jesus whose corporate personality was initially brought home to him in his Damascus conversion. With Paul the Christian shares the present joyful relation with the risen Lord, and labors amid difficulty to bring creation closer to the future manifestation of the Lord's full parousia. Paul expresses this with rhetorical drama and eloquence in Romans 8:18–39.

The second most important function attributed to Jesus is that of servant. Jesus was the suffering servant of whom Deutero-Isaiah spoke. The messianic interpretation of the suffering servant before the time of Christ has been well established.[116] Even if this were still disputed, it remains abundantly and forcefully evident that the NT witnesses and writers interpreted Jesus' life, passion, and resurrection in terms of the innocent servant who suffers vicariously to expiate the sins of others. This, above all, was the way Jesus saw and explained the meaning and significance of his own life and death.[117]

There are at least seven linguistic, literary, and thematic parallels to the suffering servant of Deutero-Isaiah in the Philippians hymn. One of the most striking is the statement "he emptied himself," which corresponds to "he poured out his life" in Is 53:12. This same thought of surrendering life is carried by the language reflecting the Eucharistic words of Jesus, "this is my body which is *given* for you," Luke 22:19, and "this is my blood of the covenant which is *poured out* for many," Mark 14:24. The suffering servant motif helps Paul and the evangelists more deeply penetrate the meaning of the remarkable events preceding and following the death of Jesus. For Paul, the suffering servant mystery explains his own vocation to join those whom he formerly persecuted, to preach, labor, suffer, ultimately to die, in order to be with the Lord always. Later in the Philippian letter, 3:10, Paul speaks of

116. Zimmerli and Jeremias, *Servant of God*, 43–79.

117. Ibid., 103–6.

the relationship of his present suffering with Christ's suffering, cf. also 2 Cor 1:5; Rom 8:17. Elsewhere he does not explicitly refer to Christ's death in the language of his suffering. The apostle himself becomes "the suffering servant." For the Christian, this aspect of the Christ mystery opens our understanding to the meaning of the painful human situation of life. The authentic Christian is called to be a "suffering servant."

The third frequent title that Jesus used of himself was Son of Man. There is still quite a bit of discussion about the various strata of these sayings, those concerning the coming of the Son of Man, those concerning his activity on earth, and those concerning the suffering and rising of the son of man.[118] However there is a strong historical core which links these allusions to the transcendent corporate personality of Daniel with the corporate personality of the suffering servant.[119] There is adequate evidence to show that similar links are present in the Philippians hymn.

Paul presupposes the pre-existence of Christ, which is related to the apocalyptic Son of Man tradition. The pre-existence of Christ enables Paul to understand the place of the Lord before all creation and as the head and cornerstone of the church. For the Christian, this is the person who is so close to the Father that he did his work and spoke his Words so that we all could address him: *Abba*.

The fourth notable title or theme attributed to Jesus is the role of the New Adam or the Second Adam. If the hymn is pre-Pauline, then the lines of this New-Adam understanding of Jesus may likewise be pre-Pauline. However there are many strands of the Genesis tradition in the NT which seem to parallel the New-Adam typology without definitely stating it in those terms; Christ as the image and likeness of God, and the new creation, and the new paradise themes. The hymn expresses the choice of Jesus not

118. Todt, *Son of Man*.

119. deFraine, *Adam and Family*; J. Robinson, "Historicality of Biblical Language."

to covet, not to desire "to be like God," but to "become obedient all the way to death" as a strong reversal of the situation attributed to the first Adam.

For Paul, the dying of Jesus and the resurrection from the dead is the baptismal source of our "new life" Rom 6; 1 Cor 15:21–22. For the Christian, this means the closer that we share in the paschal death-resurrection mystery the more closely we share in the free gift of life that is the Trinity. This two-fold dynamic of Christ, who freely chose the human situation of self-surrender and death and who rose from the dead for us, is the central reality of the Christian life and the underlying inspiration of the Philippians hymn.

Christ's obedience to death is expressed in other terms in the NT, sometimes in relation to doing the work of his Father, as in John, sometimes as fulfilling what was necessary for his resurrection.[120] It is interesting to notice how Paul applies this redemptive dialectic of death and resurrection to the inner dynamics of his own life and faith. David Stanley demonstrated how Paul applied the role of the suffering servant to himself.[121] Speaking of the risen body he says: "It is sown in weakness, it is raised in power," 1 Cor 15:43; and of himself when reflecting on his personal life of suffering, "My grace is sufficient for you, for my power is made perfect in weakness," 2 Cor 12:9; "For when I am weak, then I am strong," 2 Cor 12:10; "He is not weak in dealing with you, but is powerful in you. For he was crucified in weakness, but lives by the power of God. For we are weak in him, but in dealing with you we shall live with him by the power of God," 2 Cor 13:3–4. What was true for Christ becomes a reality for Paul and applies to all Christians who are the body of this representative Person. Faith is the life of obedience to the dialectical struggle between weakness and power. By it

120. The expression of necessity in *dei*, *edei* occurs frequently in key passages: Acts 3:18; 4:12; 9:16; 14:22; 17:3, 10; 13:27–29; John 3:14; 12:34; Mk 16:21; Matt 16:21; Luke 9:22; 17:25; 24:7, 26, 46; 26:35.

121. Stanley, *Apostolic Church in New Testament*, 337–51.

we are introduced to Christ and incorporated into Christ because we die and rise with him in Baptism. The life of dynamic tension is carried out by obedience to the Holy Spirit who moves us away from our self-centeredness to the other-centered Christ life, a life directed by the Holy Spirit (Rom 8).

There have been attempts to isolate and then interpret the kenosis of Phil 2:7 as an emptying of the divinity of Christ.[122] Kenoticism is the polar opposite of docetism and is based on an incomplete theological understanding of the central message of revelation. Also, from what we have seen of the meaning behind the language of the hymn, it is based on an incomplete exegesis of the full meaning of the passage. Kenosis itself is another way to express the Incarnation and invites the Christian to a life of self-giving.

The present Roman Catholic liturgy places the Philippians hymn in liturgies that memorialize the passion and death of Christ. It is read before the Matthean Passion on Palm Sunday, a liturgy that dates from at least the end of the fourth century, and the prediction of the passion in John 12:31–36 on September 12, the feast of the Exaltation of the Holy Cross, seventh century, and with the prediction of the passion in Matt 20:17–19 in the votive Mass of the Holy Cross, Alcuin (d. 804).

Finally, in calling the whole church to holiness, the Second Vatican Council concludes chapter five of *Lumen Gentium*, the "Constitution on the Church," with an appeal to that perfect form of charity manifested in Jesus Christ, "the man for others."

> The Church also keeps in mind the advice of the Apostle who summoned the faithful to charity by exhorting them to share the mind of Christ Jesus—He who "emptied himself taking the nature of a slave . . . becoming obedient to death (Phil 2:7–8), and, because of us, "being rich he became poor" (2 Cor 8:9).[123]

122. Taylor, *Person of Christ*, 260–76; Beare, *Commentary on Philippians*, 159–74.

123. #42 Abbott, *Documents of Vatican II*, 72.

The first half of the Philippians hymn is also used in the "Decree on Ecumenism" for an appeal that every Christian participate in the church's self-reformation so that Christ might be transparent in her.

> Every Catholic must therefore aim at Christian perfection (Jas 1:4; Rom 12:1–2) and, each according to his station, play his part so that the Church, which bears in her own body the humility and dying of Jesus (2 Cor 4:10; Phil 2:5–8) may daily be more purified and renewed, against the day when Christ will present her to Himself in all her glory, without spot or wrinkle (Eph 5:27).[124]

For the impact of the hymn on the Second Vatican Council, see Table 2.[125]

Table 2. References to the Philippians hymn in
The Documents of Vatican II

Philippians	Vatican II Document	Paragraph	Page
2:5	Laity	33	521
2:5–8	Ecumenism	4	348
2:6*	Church	8	23
2:7*	Missions	24	614
2:7–8*	Religious Life	14	476
2:7–8	Religious Life	5	470
2:7–8*	Church	42	72
2:7–9*	Priests	15	565
2:8	Religious Life	1	467
2:8–9	Church	36	62
2:8–10	Church	42	72 FN

*direct quote

In the experience of its "growing pains," the church today, pope, bishops, priests, religious, laity, the whole ecclesial family

124. #4 Abbott, *Documents of Vatican II*, 348–49.

125. Compiled from Whelan, "Index of Scripture in Vatican II," 1975–90.

of the baptized, can hear something very revealing in Phil 2:5–11. Suffering Israel of the exile began to understand the meaning of its fate through the prophetic words and actions of Jeremiah and Ezekiel. Deutero-Isaiah transposed the experience of loss and exilic suffering to the image of a servant, the servant of Yahweh. The remnant believers and the later spiritual *anawim*/"poor" or "humble" who heard and received this word, understood how serious Yahweh was about his covenant. He finally touched their hearts directly through the meekness, suffering, and hopefulness of the prophetic symbol of the servant. This direct approach by the prophet that appeals to elements common to human experience was to bear the influence that the military resistance of a powerful earthly king, "even when this king does justice to the poor," could not do.[126]

Human maturity grows out of situations that we do not create, but that we accept, negotiate, and make our own. These encountered situations eventually lead us to redirect our dominant choices. The result is a challenge to respond, address, and reshape further situations that were not a consequence of our original or dominant choice. The interchange of action, passion and response seem to belong to the earthly experience of Jesus' "self-emptying," a free and dominant choice to follow the prophetic role to which he was called by his Father, that entailed suffering and ultimate sacrifice in love and obedience for others. This seems to be the kind of service toward which the church's head and servant-leader is inviting all Christians to respond today. Kingship, power, rule, triumphal resurrection, and perfect unity come later for those who have faith in Christ. The Holy Spirit seems to be calling the individual Christian and directing the whole church today towards a new creation of the Christian order in which the basic attitude can be sketched from the gospel: loving service and obedient self-sacrifice for others. Such was the attitude of Christ celebrated in the Philippians hymn.

126. Schoonenberg, "He Emptied Himself," 62.

UPDATE

Nearly forty-five years of scholarship separate this present essay from the current state of New Testament research. My studies of a kenotic influence on Paul Tillich and comparison with Zen Buddhist "emptying" only marginally touched research on Phil 2.

One semester while teaching Old Testament and New Testament to Dominican College undergraduates, I prepared an annotated bibliography on "the servant" theme. Besides OT and NT resources on the "servant," I added studies in Christology, Ecclesiology, Spirituality, Ministry/Work, and Sacrifice/Expiation. During nearly four decades, teaching twenty-four credit hours a year, with an average of six different preparations each year, with no major or minor in Religious Studies, reading book reviews was the most I could do to keep abreast of ongoing research on Phil 2.

Publications by Ralph P. Martin and John Reumann on Phil 2:5–11 offer the major contributions to this update. Martin's book on Phil 2:5–11 was published in 1967, but was not available when I completed my research. Later, reading this work of Martin, I realized his book did professionally what my essay treated as a beginner.

Four things stand out in Martin's 1967 book, *Carmen Christi*. First, he includes extensive research into the past forty years of publications on the Philippians hymn, many among German Lutheran scholars. Secondly, he sorts out and explains alternative viewpoints regarding the major purpose and function of the hymn, ethical, soteriological, liturgical, and polemical. Thirdly, he offers new suggestions regarding its origins.

Martin favors the view that the Phil 2 hymn arose from missionary members of the school of the martyred Stephen who came to operate out of the early Christian community in Antioch (Acts 11:19 ff). He provides eight reasons why Stephen's followers are candidates for authorship of the hymn. They include the new universality of the Jewish Christian mission, the language links between Stephen's speech in Acts 7 and Phil 2; the Syrian base in

Antioch for Hellenistic, Jewish Christians; similar images of Christ in the letter to the Hebrews with regard to "a *katabasis* into this world, and a return to the celestial world."[127]

Fourth, Martin cites Gilbert Murray, *Five Stages of Greek Religion*,[128] to explain the overall anxiety of the Hellenistic mind in the first century AD, during which "religion entered upon a phase of pessimism and despair. The scientists had given an important place to the stars and planets in the systems."[129] This stage gave rise to pagan cults which promised escape from "Necessity (*anankē*) and Destiny (*heimarmenē*)."[130]

E. R. Dodds called the second and third centuries of Hellenistic cultural and religious history, "an Age of Anxiety."[131] Dodds borrowed the label from the title of W. H. Auden's play by that name. Dodds carefully detailed the voices of anxious writers from Marcus Aurelius to Constantine, who commented on the miseries of life in the material, demonic, and divine worlds.[132] Martin says Hellenistic people "craved a freedom from the power or tyranny of evil spirits. . . . They cried out for some mighty god who would . . . deliver them from bondage" to cruel fate, and the unfair rule of necessity and destiny. The soul sought redemption from estrangement in a sinful, finite, mortal body.[133] In Phil 2:10–11, these forces bow down in submissive worship to the pioneer who breaks through our common human bondage.

Finally, Martin summarizes the work of Dieter Georgi (1964) that claimed "the hymn utilizes the framework of the Sophia-myth but reinterprets it in the light of the early Hellenistic Jewish claim

127. R. Martin, *Carmen Christi*, 305 n. 8.

128. R. Martin, *Carmen Christi*.

129. Ibid., 307.

130. Ibid., 308.

131. Dodds, *Age of Anxiety*.

132. Smith and Lounibos, *Pagan and Christian Anxiety*.

133. R. Martin, *Carmen Christi*, 309.

that placed Jesus on a par with Yahweh as Lord of the world."[134] The pattern of Jesus' mission as an "embodiment of divine wisdom . . . in space and time . . . [in] humiliation and exaltation, [is] based on the presentation of the wise, righteous man in the Wisdom literature."[135]

In my view, the wisdom motif is much more prominent in John's Gospel, from the prologue onward. *Sophia/Hokma* is very close to John's use of *Logos,* the Word. In "the Word became flesh and dwelt among us" John 1:14, we can hear, "the wise one, the person who knows and does justice, entered our space and time to teach us how to live according to God's true love and justice for the world." Hints of the wise servant are contained in the hymn's self-emptying, becoming human, obedient to God's plan.

As an interlude, Michael Gordon contributes linguistic narrative patterns to his study of Phil 2:5–11, which he calls "Paul's Master Story."[136] He divides the first half of the hymn into a threefold rhetorical pattern (1) narrative, (2) semantic, (3) syntactic: "although" 2:6a [x], "not" 2:6b [y], "but" 2:7–8 [z]. "Although he was in the form of God, he did not exploit equality with God, but emptied/ humbled himself." Gordon finds this threefold rhetorical pattern in other Pauline passages, namely, 2 Cor 8:9; Rom 15:1–3; 1 Thess 2:6–8; 1 Cor 11:1. The pattern takes the form: x=status, y=not selfish act, z=but selfless acts.[137] Gordon's purpose is to move Pauline thought from *kenōsis*, through justification, to *theōsis*. He boldly asserts, "*Kenōsis* is *theōsis*. To be like Christ crucified is to be both not godly and most human. Christification is divinization, and divinization is humanization."[138]

John Reumann published the Anchor Bible Commentary on *Philippians* in 2008. This series offers a gold standard of English

134. Ibid., 318.

135. Ibid., 319.

136. Gorman, *Inhabiting the Cruciform God*, 9.

137. Ibid., 16–17.

138. Ibid., 37.

language commentaries on all books of the Bible. After decades of writing and research, Reumann's first draft came to 2,800 pages. The published book is 805 pp, with citations from over 3,000 scholars. "Phil 2:6–11 has long been the Mount Everest of Philippians study,"[139] Reumann writes. He makes a good Sherpa, guiding us up the mountain. The difficulty of the climb is the big crowd of climbers and their baggage at the base camp.

Reumann's approach is more historical than literary. Describing Philippi when Paul began his mission there in AD 48–49 (Acts 16:11–40), the city had 10,000 inhabitants within 167 acres of walled city and 700 square miles of suburbs. Philippi was founded and named after Philip II of Macedon in 358–357 BC near Krenides, "Tiny Spring." It was a gold-mining area.[140] Later it was intersected by the Roman road, Via Egnatia, which ran from the Adriatic to the Aegean sea. It became a Roman colony of military veterans after 42 BC. Reumann calls it a "little Rome" because it had self-governance, citizen's rights, and tax exemptions.[141] Its cultural and religious layers were Thracian, Hellenistic, with a dominance of "*Romanitas*" topped off by "Imperial religion and the Emperor cult."[142] Reumann holds that "Jews were negligible or nonexistent[143] in Roman Philippi."[144] His reason is that "Acts 16 and archeology report no synagogue (at best a 'place of prayer' for a few women like Lydia, a convert)."[145] Fitzmyer holds the more traditional view that there was "a small settlement of Jews in the town,[146] and "a contingent of Diaspora Jews."[147] The issue of ethnic

139. Reumann, *Philippians, A New Translation*, 333.

140. Fitzmyer, *Acts*, 584.

141. Ibid., 3; Fitzmyer, *Acts of the Apostles*, 584.

142. Reumann, *Philippians, A New Translation*, 4.

143. Bockmuehl, 9.

144. Reumann, *Philippians, A New Translation*, 4.

145. Ibid., 4.

146. Fitzmyer, *Acts of the Apostles*, 247.

147. Ibid., 584.

background for the Philippian population whom Paul evangelized, which began with Lydia and the unnamed jailer and their households in Acts 16, and those who received his letter(s) is important. After all "Paul established his first European Christian community there."[148]

To judge from the names of his converts, Lydia, Euodia, Syntyche, Epaphroditus, Syzygus, and Clement, the Philippian house-church was predominantly Gentile.[149] Reumann writes "Phil may echo but never overtly quotes (OT) Scripture ([4] Comment A. 1)."[150] Commenting on Phil 1:19, Reumann qualifies his "echo" by saying "all OT wordings in Phil are 'embedded,' not cited . . . no formula shows Scripture is being quoted."[151] Reumann's conclusion that Jewish converts were absent among Paul's original audience and recipients of his letter(s) to the household churches in Philippi, allows him to interpret Phil 2:6–11 as a passage of Greco-Roman rhetoric without any explicit OT references.

That is one reason Reumann claims Phil 2:6–11 is not a liturgical hymn, but as he calls it, "an *encomion* (Latin *encomium*)," a statement of high praise, or an expression of "epideictic rhetoric."[152] It is part of indigenous Christian missionary polemics against pagan worship of imperial heroes and gods.[153] Reumann thinks the passage was composed by Philippian Christians "as a tool for missionary outreach, to evangelize Roman culture by people who lived in it, and so advance the gospel (1:5, 12, 27), reworking what they had learned from Paul in idioms of their own."[154] So the work is para-Pauline, not pre-Pauline, and was brought to Paul in Ephesus

148. Ibid., 247.

149. Ibid.

150. Reumann, *Philippians, A New Translation*, 4.

151. Ibid., 232.

152. Ibid., 361, 4.

153. Ibid., 363–35.

154. Ibid., 362–63.

by Epaphroditus.[155] This is the reconstruction of a good historical imagination, one way to revisit and reengage the past. Reumann's conclusions draw from reams of contemporary NT scholarship.

Phil 2:5–11 manifests a downward and an upward movement, called *katabasis* and *anabasis* in Greek.[156] This is one among more than twenty views offered to interpret the passage over centuries of commentary. *Phroneite* (1:7; 2:2, 5 and 4:10 "your concern for me" which is a "Philippian slogan") connotes "thoughtful conduct and a life with discernment (about citizenship in [the] *polis* and [in] church groups), as well as the relationship of baptized believers to Christ and to God signified in *touto*."[157]

Drawing from recent NT studies, Reumann concludes the view of J. Jeremias that interpreted "he emptied himself" 2:7a as derived from Is 53:12 "the servant poured himself out to death" ". . . has been widely rejected as background."[158] "The attempt to make 'he emptied himself of life,' by death (Is 53:12, a [suffering] Servant background) is unlikely; death is mentioned specifically at 8b; therefore premature at 7a."[159] Reumann not only cast out allusions to the suffering servant of Isaiah 53 but, with other scholars, dismisses allusions to a new Adam or Son of Man tradition in the encomium, even more so any clues of ancient Gnostic or pagan divine-man myths.[160]

Finally, Reumann translated *doulos* 2:7, not as servant but as slave, to emphasize the "ownership of a human being," or the slave to fate and the powers of the world as in Gal 4:8–9. "To be equal to God" 2:6 "was an ancient [pagan] aim and goal."[161] *Morphē*/"form," 6a, 7b is not philosophy "but popular language average people in

155. Ibid., 365.
156. Ibid., 335.
157. Ibid., 375.
158. Ibid., 348, 361.
159. Ibid., 367–68.
160. Ibid., 333–39.
161. Ibid., 367.

Philippi might use."[162] It meant a "'mode of existence,' sphere, or realm where a person is."[163]

John Reumann, Ralph Martin, and other selected authors offer some research updates on Philippians 2:5–11. Martin develops material along the lines begun in this paper. Reumann, who represents present scholarly consensus in his interpretations, offers what might be called a "secular hypothesis" about inhabitants of first-century Philippi. The absence of Jewish converts in the Philippi church, renders Paul's entire letter unique, as if in this letter Paul avoided using his customary Old Testament midrash, and instead consciously shaped it to address a formerly pagan Greek and Roman audience.

What has happened to the likes of Lydia, the Gentile woman from Bythinia, who joined Jewish people at Philippi in Sabbath prayer, remains for future scholars to uncover. Perhaps her household celebrated baptisms and Eucharists and composed the hymn to Christ for her house liturgies. If she and her companions knew more about Jewish traditions than Reumann claims, future Philippian studies may reshape a synthesis of literary and historical traditions behind the hymn. I commend Reumann for his mastery of massive research and erudite insights. His view from the summit of Mount Everest remains cloudy for this climber.

There is a music, a cadence, a poetic sensibility to the prayerful public anamnesis and communal memory of Jesus as Lord. An encomium usually represents the voice of one person in praise of another. The Philippians hymn sounds like many voices sung in harmony. It represents a Christian aesthetic of faith and hope deep enough to change the hearts of its Philippian hearers who serve one another in acts of selfless love. Phil 2:5–11 obviously ends in praise of Jesus Christ as Lord. But it proclaims a conversion, a huge turn-around for our humble human condition. It is the whole Jesus story put to the music of praise.

162. Ibid.

163. Ibid.

PART II

Paul Tillich's Kenotic Tendency

INTRODUCTION

THE EXISTENCE of fragments from a kenotic Christology in the theology of Paul Tillich (1886–1965) does not imply that his works frequently drew upon the biblical text of Philippians 2:5–11. Nor does it claim to situate Tillich in one or the other of the nineteenth-century kenosis camps in European, Protestant theological debate.[1]

Kenosis stands for the expression in Philippians 2:7 "he emptied himself," *heauton ekenōsen*, or as the *New English Bible* translates it, "He made himself nothing." Kenotic as it is used in this essay refers to a theological tendency to interpret the mystery of Christ by means of a particular understanding of self-emptying.

1. Significant work on the history of the exegesis of Phil 2:5–11 has been done by Henry, "*Kénose*," 7–161; Grelot "*La traduction*," 897–922 and 1009–26; Loofs, "Kenosis," *Realencyklopedie*, 246–63; Loofs "Kenosis," *Hastings*, 680–87. Some modern versions were reviewed by Pannenberg, *Jesus*, 307–23. Biblical perspectives have been offered by Jeremias, *Zu Phil 2.7*, 182–88; R. Martin, *Carmen Christi*; Feuillet, *"l'Hymne,"* 352–80 and 481–507; Taylor, *Person of Christ*, 260–78. Thomasius and the Erlangen position was summarized by Welch, *Protestant Thought*, 233–40. For kenosis as the basis of sacred-profane dialectic, see Altizer and Hamilton, *Radical Theology*, 140–55. Dawe, *Form of a Servant*, offers a historical summary and a kenotic theology of personal love and limiting freedom distinct from the Hellenistic and idealistic versions.

Tillich's Christology has drawn more or at least sharper criticism than any other part of his theology. Gustave Weigel, SJ, was one of the first American theologians to spot a Nestorian tendency in Tillich's Christology, especially after the publication in 1950 of "A Reinterpretation of the Doctrine of the Incarnation."[2]

George Tavard, who has given Tillich's Christology a long look in *Paul Tillich and the Christian Message*, wrote in 1962: "Between 1949 and 1957, the date of *Systematic Theology II*, his doctrine has not evolved. . . . From the point of view of Christian orthodoxy, it is just as weak now as it was then."[3] The examination of Tillich's kenotic tendency does not intend to add to the list of heresies already alleged against Tillich's Christology. It offers a historical background that seems necessary to understand Tillich's Christ. It claims that Tillich's interest in Schelling's late thought included the adoption of a "Kenotic Christology" which became a principle for theological interpretation of Christian revelation.

FRIEDRICH W. J. SCHELLING

Paul Tillich wrote two dissertations on the work of the German idealist and romantic philosopher, Friedrich Wilhelm Joseph Schelling, the first at the University of Breslau in 1910 on the role of myth and revelation in history, and the second at the University of Halle in 1912 on Schelling's ideas of mysticism and guilt. Tillich frequently called Schelling the first existentialist. Schelling's father was a Lutheran Semitic scholar who wrote commentaries on the Old Testament when he taught at the seminary located in the former Cistercian abbey at Bebenhausen, near Stuttgart in Swabia.

2. Tillich, "Reinterpretation of Incarnation," 133–48; Weigel, "Contemporary Protestantism," 177–202.

3. Tavard, Paul Tillich, 129. The same point is recalled by W. and M. Pauck, *Tillich Life and Thought*, 243. The first comparative study of Catholic thought and Paul Tillich was published by O'Meara and Weisser, *Tillich in Catholic Thought*. One of the finest introductions to Frederick Schelling's thought and influence on Catholic thought in the nineteenth century is O'Meara, *Romantic Idealism and Roman Catholicism*.

That the thought of the later Schelling dealt with a kenotic Christology seems unmistakable. Walter Kasper summarized the significance of Christology in the work of the later Schelling.[4] For Schelling, Christ is the content, *Inhalt*, of Christianity.[5] This is not a Kantian ideal, *Inbegriff*, but a historical content. Nor is it to be identified with Hegel's absolute becoming incarnate in history. It is a unique historical act and event, *Christusereignis als Geschehen*, which follows from the doctrine of the Trinity which was reconstructed from the background of Schelling's earlier transcendental idealism into a formula for the trinitarian economy by a quasi-ontological succession of potencies, the unfolding of the subjectivity of God into history.

Kasper distinguished Schelling's kenotic Christology from the mid-nineteenth-century versions of the European schools. It had Reformation origins inasmuch as the dispute concerning the Lord's Supper forced Martin Luther to interpret the communication of idioms of the divine properties to the human nature of Christ, *Ubiquitats Lehre*. Kasper suggested that Schelling could have heard the "cryptic kenosis" theory of the Tübingen school from his teacher G. Storr. But Schelling rejected both the hidden divinity thesis, which had a docetic tendency, as well as the non-use interpretation of the Geissen theologians. For Schelling, kenosis did not refer to pre-existence but to the historical incarnation. "According to Schelling the kenosis concerns not a being-change, or a being decrease, but a condition change, a distinct standing of Christ. . . . The form of God does not mean the divine essence, but its there being, *Daseinform*, in the Lordship."[6]

In the process of the trinitarian processions there can be a non-temporal successive revelation of each person. Thus the "in the form of God" is something other than the divine essence; it is the external species of God, which consists at least in the Lordship,

4. Kasper, *Das Absolute in Geschichte*, 369–411.

5. Ibid., 369–71.

6. Ibid., 370–77.

as dominion over being.[7] This is the position of the Son at the end of the mythological process in history where, at least for human consciousness, he is Lord of being.[8] In successive, ongoing revelation, the Son is no longer concealed in the nature potency as a cosmic nature-Lord. Kenosis for Schelling meant de-glorifying, *Entherrlichung,* and de-mystifying, *Entzauberung*, the world, not a negation of the divine essence, but a negation of the external, divine sublimity in which the Logos knows itself as man and freely submits himself to God.[9] This is the end of the pagan religion and mythology and the purpose of revelation because all darkness has been removed. Kenosis is not a veiling of divinity but its revelation in obedience, creatureliness and the Cross of the man Jesus Christ. It is the self-liberation of the true divinity, and a destruction of false veils of cosmic Lordship that concealed his true divinity.

Schelling no longer returned to Luther's theology of the Cross from the Heidelberg disputation: *Non ille digne Theologus dicitur, qui invisibilia Dei per ea, quae facta sunt, intellecta conspicit, sed qui visibilia et posteriora Dei per passiones et crucem conspecta intelligit.*[10] "A person worthy of the title theologian is not the one who finds the invisible God through created realities, but rather the one who understands that God is found by perceiving the visible effects of God through sufferings and the cross" (author's translation). God is hidden in suffering; in Christ God is covered, clothed, veiled yet manifested. On the other hand, one who seeks God from outside finds the devil. For Luther, every arbitrary invention of God comes to that end. Schelling knows he cannot invent God, but must wait until God draws him, which he does in the obedience of Christ under the appearance of a stranger, *sub specie aliena.* God's irony is that he reveals himself through contradiction—in

7. Ibid., 377.
8. Ibid., 377–78.
9. Ibid., 378.
10. Ibid., 379.

weakness is strength—and here it is that Schelling understands God's freedom.[11]

Luther's Christology taught that God is only concrete for us in Christ, *intra*. This led to the conclusion that the Logos can only be encountered in flesh, Christ Incarnate. This seemed to deny God's freedom. But the reformed alternative of the Logos entirely within and without the flesh, *totus intra et extra*, opened the gate for every possible speculation about the *Logos-a-sarkikos*. Schelling tried to solve this difficulty by a there-being-way, *Daseinweise*, an interpretation of time that focused upon an interpretation of John's prologue. Time is God's way of being present, eternity is his overcoming time, begun in the incarnation. In his becoming in time, God shows his freedom from time. The freedom of God is shown in its self-limitation. God is not pure antinomy or contradiction, although his sovereignty can be shown in contradiction. God is so infinite and free that he is in the finitude of infinity, free in obedience, and Lord in self-abasement.[12]

Günter Sommer examined Schelling's kenotic Christology and reached general conclusions similar to Kasper's. In his thesis on Schelling and Tillich, Sommer holds that Schelling's kenotic Christology resulted from an application of the theory of potencies to a theory of the history of religious myth.

> Thus it seems that Schelling knows ultimately only one nature, and yet, may speak of two, in that nature in its "being-basis," *Basis-Sein*, is a divine reality; only in its externality is it potentially demonic, and only in its arousal through man can it become actually demonic. This point of view was at the heart of Schelling's (and also Tillich's) transformation of the two-nature theory. Schelling distinguished his theory from all preceding theories by saying: "Christ is indeed *in duabus*, but not *ex duabus naturis*."[13]

11. Kasper, *Das Absolute in Geschichte*, 380. The importance of freedom in Schelling's work is revisited by Bracken, "Freedom and Causality," 164–82.

12. Tavard, *Paul Tillich*, 380–81.

13. Sommer, "Significance of Schelling for Tillich," 130.

Nature for Schelling and for Tillich is in God, subsisting, eternally overcoming non-being, the first potency, the basis for the divine dialectic. In the fall of man, the end of the mythological period, non-being achieved an external, actual cosmic status. Satan became ruler of the world. Schelling's satanology is the background for the kenotic Christology as it expressed an objectification of the first potency in creation. "Christ in his cosmic form of independence, *morphē Theou,* did not grasp, *Harpagmos,* the *dynamis* [power] which Satan offered."[14] Christ renounced the extra-divine, mythic form, to permit his essential divinity to become manifest through a human subject. "In the death of Jesus 'the divine broke through the natural.'"[15] A structured reality replaced the unstructured chaotic principle, called the first potency by the early Schelling, and prepared for the appearance of the Spirit.

Sommer maintained that a remnant of Schelling's kenotic Christology is essentially present and functional in Tillich's doctrine of final revelation. "The absolute side of the final revelation, that in it which is unconditional and unchangeable, involves the complete transparency and the complete self-sacrifice of the medium in which it appears."[16] Sommer[17] argued that the paschal mystery of Christ's death and resurrection is implicit in Tillich's correlation between his ontology and his theology of final revelation, and in the correlation between dynamics and form which provides for the appearance of the Spirit, ". . . which means for Schelling that human consciousness is spiritual and free. Tillich has replaced Schelling's speculative, scriptural-mythological ontology with strictly ontological terms."[18] Although the ontological language has changed, the kenotic substance remains the same.

14. Ibid., 132.

15. Ibid.

16. Tillich, *ST*, 151. Tillich used the metaphor of "transparency" for the early versions of the Gestalt of Grace in Tillich, *The Protestant Era,* 212.

17. Sommer, "Significance of Schelling for Tillich," 134.

18. Ibid., 147–48.

SELF-EMPTYING OF CHRIST AND THE CHRISTIAN

TILLICH & SCHELLING

The first time Tillich explicitly acknowledged Schelling's kenoticism was with reference to Schelling's doctrine of the potencies which explained trinitarian life *ad extra*. In his 1910 dissertation on Schelling's philosophy of religion, Tillich wrote:

> 5) the affinity with the kenotic formula which, e.g., according to Hofmann, must be shown to be directly dependent upon the Trinitarian construction cf. *Schriftbeweis, Lehrgang 2:1*: "the trinity that has become unequal to itself has posited along with its first act of self-manifestation the beginning of the historical realization of the eternal will of God."[19]

Moreover, when he explained the meaning of the biblical notion of the "Fullness of Time," Tillich again used Schelling's kenotic expression. "The fullness of time may be characterized as the moment of separateness, as the demand, *Föderung*, that the Son forsake the Lordship that he could have had independent of the Father, that is the demand that he be the Christ (*SW*, 13:37[20])."[21] The forsaking of the Lordship refers to the much disputed verse, "[who] did not consider his divine equality something to be proudly paraded" (Phil 2:6).[22] Tillich commented that the work of Christ implied in his self-sacrifice and self-surrender of all Lordship external to God, is the content of history, the essence of God's self-communication as spirit and truth.[23]

Again Tillich elaborated the relation between revealed and philosophical religion and explained the need for a moment of absolute wonder when doubt passes away and the paradox of truth

19. Tillich, *CHRS*, 164–45, n. 24. The Hofmann referred to was most likely the Erlangen disciple of Thomasius.

20. The numbers 13:37 are Tillich's citation of Schelling's *Sämtliche Werke, Vols 1–14*, Stuttgart & Augsburg, 1856–61.

21. Tillich, *CHRS*, 109. See Deeken, "*Kairos*," 113–29 for a discussion of the demand and fullness of time in early twentieth century German thought.

22. The translation is by Stanley, *Apostolic Church in New Testament*, 104.

23. Tillich, *CHRS*, 109–12.

becomes clear. Here a kenotic version of the theology of the Cross joins a dialectical synthesis of thought and action.

> The perfection of thought and that of action are equated by the act of the divine paradox: action is perfected in the principle when, in the voluntary affirmation of the Cross of Christ, the will sacrifices its own self that it posited outside of God; thought perfects itself when in the thoughtful affirmation of the cross of Christ, the dialectical process supersedes, *aufheben*, itself. The possibility for this kind of parallel consideration lies in the essence of the dialectical method, which is not subjective reflection about an object but an active rehearsal of the real process itself.[24]

Tillich rejected the Hegelian form of dialectic of the Spirit in history as the idea of superseding or sublation, the translation of *Aufhebung*. Tillich denied the progressive element in Hegel's view of history and religion, but kept the dynamism of a real dialectical sublation as an ontological version of the kenotic principle behind Christian faith within history.

In his second thesis on Schelling in 1912, Tillich studied mysticism and guilt-consciousness as constituting the concrete experience of sin and justification and as religious correlates for the philosophical principles of identity and contradiction. Commenting on the Lutheran juxtaposition of sin and grace Tillich quoted Schelling's incarnation axiom: "Only the personal can heal the personal, and God must become man in order that man may return to God."[25] Christ's self-surrender contradicts man's irrational self-contradictory will, the aroused freedom and deliberate sin of estrangement which constituted the Fall. Tillich wrote:

> The cross of Christ is the solution of this supreme contradiction, that is, the self-sacrifice and self-annulment of the will to selfhood, raised to the absolute, divine will to power. "The true infinite entered the finite, not to defy it, but to sacrifice it to God in his own person, and thereby to reconcile it (*SW*,

24. Ibid., 169 n. 14.

25. Ibid., 11.

> 5:292). . . . [T]his formulation of the significance of the incarnation grew out of the soul of the system of identity, but it has thematic significance for all periods of Schelling's development (*SW*, 14:203)."[26] The will of the contradiction that has become spiritual is at once affirmed and negated by God himself and therefore absolutely: this is the mystery of the cross and the positive solution of the problem of mysticism and guilt-consciousness.[27]

Tillich summarized his theological study of Schelling with principles derived from his philosophical thesis. Revelation is called "the religion of the conquered contradiction."[28] The grace of Christ is the theological principle of the victory and the proper effect of the kenosis.

> God assumes the form of selfhood and subjects himself to its curse so that he may have communion with those who are bound to selfhood. . . . He is completely victorious over the contradiction, by affirming it completely, by subjecting himself to it. But, because he assumes selfhood not in order to affirm it, but to deny it, therefore he sacrifices it and himself in it and thereby produces the Spirit. . . . This inner dialectic movement, from the incarnate to the crucified to the exalted—from Jesus through the Christ to the Spirit—constitutes the essence of Christianity. In this living systole and diastole the contradiction is conquered through grace and that identity is fashioned which included guilt-consciousness overcome within itself. . . It is the "religion of the Spirit and of freedom (*SW*, 14:237)."[29]

In a note to these concluding remarks about the life of the Trinity working in our history to overcome sin and lead mankind to a religion of freedom and the Spirit, Tillich explained that Schelling's idea of revelation and grace hinged on that act which designated

26. Tillich, *MGCS*, 141 n. 38.

27. Ibid., 111–12.

28. Scharlemann, "Tillich on Schelling," 107 said "the will of contradiction in this passage becomes in Tillich's later terminology 'estranged freedom.'" Tillich also calls this "aroused freedom".

29. Tillich, *MGCS*, 124–25.

Jesus' transition as incarnate to Jesus as the Christ. It is the kenotic act. "However, the Son scorns this Lordship which he could have independently of the Father, and *in this act* he is the Christ. This is the fundamental idea of Christianity (*SW*, 14:37)."[30] Schelling's idea of religion as understood by Tillich is Christocentric and Schelling's idea of the Christ center as understood by Tillich is the kenosis leading to the whole paschal mystery: death, resurrection and exaltation.

PAUL TILLICH

Tillich revisited Schelling's kenotic Christology in 1949 when he reinterpreted the Incarnation against the background of biblical mythology.

> But, we may ask, are there not indications that the biblical writers, Paul and John, describe the significance of the historical Jesus in terms of a semi-mythological character? I believe that this cannot be denied. The pre-existent spiritual being (in Phil ii.5–11) who resigns his divine form and power, and takes the form of a servant, and is raised by God on high to receive a name which is above every name—this being who makes a moral decision in his pre-existent state—is certainly not God himself, but a divine being. The decision "not to snatch at equality with God but to empty himself" occurs in a supra-historical, mythological sphere; and the same is true of his elevation to the dignity of "Lord." The distinction of the three stages is mythical, using the three modes of time for the destiny of a divine being.[31]

The christological hymn in Paul's letter to the Philippians is cited as an example of one among three mythic stages of time which reveal how the divine plan unfolds in a gradual sequence. Tillich interprets the hymnic structure and stages to represent a pre-ontological, mythic claim. On the other hand, the Johannine prologue is cited as offering an advance from myth to logos. What

30. Ibid., 143 n. 53; emphasis added.

31. Tillich, "Reinterpretation of Incarnation," 135.

Tillich wanted to show was that the biblical teaching regarding the Incarnation is not that God becomes man, "but that a divine being who represents God and is able to reveal him in his fullness, manifests himself in a form of existence which is in radical contradiction to his divine, spiritual, heavenly form."[32]

> The mythological element in the biblical doctrine of the Incarnation enabled it to be understood as the self-manifestation of God in existence through a divine half-being, half-principle which belongs to God and nevertheless shows some essentially human characteristics. The subject of the Incarnation is the original God-manhood, or the spiritual God-man, or the heavenly man, or the creative reason in which man as the image of God participates and which, therefore, is able to enlighten him.[33]

Tillich wanted to avoid the two-nature dilemma as it was argued by the Tübingen and Geissen schools of kenoticism.[34] He suggested that "the hero-cult of Arianism" led to a metaphysical rather than a soteriological Christology which his formula of essential God-manhood appearing in existence was supposed to restore.[35] The "essential God-manhood" formula intended to "translate the mythological, liturgical and numinous form of these statements into a rational and theological form.[36] The Incarnation promises essential liberation to mankind which is presently captive to an estranged condition of existence. The Incarnation is less an historical event and more an ontological transformation of the human reality which points toward a future destiny.

Tillich's soteriological Christology is a reformulation of the Pauline insight regarding the "new creature" (Gal 6:15), called the New Being. "The New Being created by the Incarnation is above essential being because it is actual and not merely potential; and

32. Ibid., 137.

33. Ibid.

34. Ibid., 138.

35. Ibid., 138–39.

36. Ibid., 139.

at the same time it is above existential being because it brings essential being or essential Godmanhood into existence."[37] In this article Tillich translated his kenotic principle inherited from Schelling into a theological formula consistent with his dramatic ontology. It is surprising how frequently the Schelling fragments within Tillich's thought regarding the meaning of time, *kairos*, the demonic, freedom, and destiny are reinterpreted in continuity with their original kenotic content and context.

In his *Systematic Theology*, several ontological dynamics and the meanings of the self, the themes of "complete transparency" and "complete self-sacrifice of the medium" of final revelation appear as remnants of an original kenotic principle. Tillich employed "transparency" as a symbol for self-surrender, love, and obedience to the Father. The redemptive act of Jesus according to Pauline theology liberates us from demonic, self-idolatrous powers which rule the world and mask as religious.

> By his crucifixion and death, Jesus rejected the worldly and demonic messianic temptations to power and meaning, thereby revealing the true Christ. For us this means that in following him we are liberated from the authority of everything finite in him, from his special traditions, from his individual piety, from his rather conditioned world view, from any legalistic understanding of his ethics. Only as the crucified is he "grace and truth" and not law. . . . Even the Christ is Christ only because he did not insist on his equality with God but renounced it as a personal possession (Phil 2)."[38]

Since Tillich found research on the historical Jesus shadowed by clouds of doubt, he demythologized the Philippians hymn to provide the first of a series of biblical symbols to corroborate the symbol of the "Cross of the Christ."[39] The same text proceeding from the dynamic of self-emptying is used to support the teach-

37. Ibid., 142. See Tillich, *ST* 2:94–96; on christological soteriology see ibid., 2:140 ff.

38. Ibid., 1:134, 147, 151.

39. Ibid., 2:158.

ings regarding pre-existence, resurrection, and eschatology.[40] Tillich's most significant interpretation of the Philippians hymn to Christ is that which rejects a Jesus-centered religion and theology for a kenotic Christology which offers a continuous self-surrender of the historical Jesus to the power of the Spirit which made him the Christ.[41]

Tillich's Christology is subordinated to a soteriology, so it is understandable that the kenotic principle led him to a kenotic spirituality, a religion of self-emptying which assisted the liberation of a person from estrangements that turn the self from the truth of the Spirit. The continuity is carried thematically by the idea of transparency which described the means for the communication of revelation to others, an attribute of saints and holy persons.[42]

A significant portion of Tillich's understanding of the human person seems to be taken from the kenotic self-emptying. This self-giving motif is carried by cognate terms like self-surrender, self-sacrifice, and self-transcendence.[43] Tillich's psychological, social, and philosophical statements about the self as center, the person as free and autonomous, in moral, cultural, and religious dimensions, are sketched on a kenotic horizon of understanding the self, which when theologically reconstructed, constituted an orientation from selfishness toward service of the divine mystery by the empowerment of the Holy Spirit.

Tillich explained "ontological asceticism" as a self-emptying of the finite, fallen, tragic elements of the encountered world, which did not try to force reunion with the infinite. A forced reunion would be a demonic distortion doomed to failure like

40. Ibid., 2:159 ff.

41. Ibid., 3:146 ff.

42. Ibid., I:121. Ford, "Tillich's Theory of Religious Symbols," 113–30 criticized the transparency theme as symbol and medium for revelation. Ford did not recognize the kenotic horizon behind this symbol and limited his view to a discussion of its philosophical adequacy. In a "Rejoinder" Tillich modified transparency with "translucency," 186–89.

43. Tillich, *ST*, 1:143, 147; 3:270–71, 392.

systems of self-salvation and other "works" formula for salvation. The divine paradox is that the transforming power of salvation, essential and actual healing in the New Being, is achieved through Christ's acceptance and sacrificial participation in our weakness, suffering, and death.[44] This happens by grace alone.[45] If what happened to Peter at his confession at Caesarea Philippi is a paradigm for what happens to the faithful Christian, then it happens by the "impact of the Spiritual Presence."[46] A kenotic spirituality requires the counter movement of Spiritual empowerment.

As late as 1963 when Tillich dialogued with students at UC Santa Barbara, he appealed to a kenotic understanding of the Christ.

> Student: Well, I'm still puzzled because I would like to know what the relation is between Jesus and ourselves and other men. Is Jesus unique only because history or historical factors converge in a certain way—in a uniquely significant way—at the time of his life?
>
> Dr. Tillich: No, no, no! I have now given already at least three answers to this. My chief answer was the lack of any "scar" which would show an estrangement from God. That is one thing. Another was the total self-sacrifice of "him who is the Christ"; for the Messiah can be the Messiah only if he sacrifices his finitude. That was the second answer. The third answer was that he shows the presence, in his sufferings and on the cross, of an utter humility. He humiliates himself as a slave and experiences the death of a slave. Now this demonstrates that God is not strange to the lowest reality.[47]

The essentially free person, a new creature, familiar, not a stranger, to God, could only be recreated by means of the dialectic

44. Ibid., 2:174–76.

45. Ibid., 2:178–79.

46. Ibid., 3:150.

47. D. Brown, *Ultimate Concern*, 155–56. Tillich also mentioned the nearness of Jesus to the prophecy of Isaiah 53, ibid., 57, and the heavenly glory of Phil 2, ibid., 215.

of self-affirmation and self-denial which prepared the way for authentic Christian self-transcendence. In Schelling's paraphrase of the Gospel, "The seed of corn of our wisdom must die and must disappear in unwisdom, so that from this death and this nothingness the life and being of a higher knowledge may spring forth and be created anew."[48]

CONCLUSION

The tendency of nineteenth-century romantic idealism that searched for transcendence through subjective understanding, was partly balanced by a Christian perspective, at least on the part of F. W. J. Schelling, with the incarnation taken as a principle of self-emptying, so that no finite reality, not even the earthly humanity of the historical Jesus, much less any earthly institutions like church or state, least of all reason or the self, was adequate for receiving or understanding the mystery of God's self-communication to humanity through Christ. For Tillich and Schelling, the scandal of finitude was expressed radically in Jesus' self-emptying, and signaled the historical end of mythic religions and the unique *kairos* or time for revealed religion. The self-emptying of Jesus operated as a concrete, objective Christian norm against which the transcendental subjectivity of idealist thought was critiqued. The Pauline version of the redemptive mystery of the Cross was translated by Tillich into an ontological reality principle in order to understand what was final, perfect, designed to completely overcome our many estrangements by the revelation and symbol of the Christ.

As it moved into the twentieth century, the significance of the kenotic principle was not so much the distance it placed between itself and the total Pauline context or the Chalcedon formulas; an expanded kenotic principle gave all revelation a humanist orientation and kept future and final revelation in suspense. It challenged

48. Tillich, *CHRS*, 114.

Christians to forge a responsible discipleship out of their limited uses of finite freedom. The move from a self-centered autonomy, against and beyond the daily demons of heteronomy, takes a faith and courage to confront, expose, and empty the non-being of false desires and designs for humanity. The kenotic principle aligns with the radical prophetic principle that analyzes and judges the demonic as well as the *kairos* in history to uncover pathways for the positive renewal of humanity in the world under the guiding presence of the Holy Spirit. That Tillich envisioned such a spiritual mission seems evident from the multiple roles he attributed to the Spirit in Volume III of *Systematic Theology*.[49]

If the preceding analysis of Tillich's kenotic tendency has been correct, questions arise about some of its practical consequences. To the extent that thinking in Christ or having the mind of Christ (Phil 2:5) is represented by an emphasis on self-emptying, by that same proportion is there an accompanying diminishment of the capacity of the free, thinking subject to discern which spirit in oneself and the world comes from God and leads toward God? What formative or transforming contribution can the responsible Christian make toward consecrating the world for and in Christ, if the fundamental spiritual representation of Christ in time is form-emptying? Does the emphasis on a kenotic sense of Christian sacrifice and the cross in a Christian-oriented life in juxtaposition with a powerful surge toward an objective direction for transcendental subjectivity, place a tension on these two seemingly polar opposite tendencies, that tempts one toward Stoicism or mystical

49. Reisz, "Ambiguities," 89–103 distinguishes "God as Spirit," "The Spiritual Presence" and "Spirit as Divine Life". He offers a formal and instrumental distinction to explain the first two designations of the Spirit who is the source or cause of divine grace in us. Tillich used spirit as an analogue for human experience, e.g., *ST* 3:22); perhaps part of the ambiguity of Spirit may be traceable to Hegel's use of *Geist*. Quentin Lauer offered at least five possible meanings for Hegel's *Geist*: 1) absolute spirit, 2) each individual spirit, 3) the spirit of a people or an age, 4) a universal idea, 5) a combination of all four above. See 4. The affinities between Hegel's *Geist* and Tillich's Spirit are countered in part by his use of Schelling's kenotic Christology.

quietude? Finally, does Tillich's kenotic tendency ultimately join the larger stream of nineteenth-century kenotic Christologies, consciously and unconsciously applied to ecclesiology in such a way that it supports a tendency toward religious socialism, which, in the search for a newly centered society, has rejected every heteronomy, overcoming estrangements, all self-centered social structures, and most dominant social forms?

Some of these questions arise from study of the kenotic pattern of Russian thought and spirituality which Nadejada Gorodetzky and George P. Fedotov have traced in Russian fiction and spiritual, moral, and doctrinal writings from Kievan Christianity to the end of the nineteenth century.[50] The kenotic pattern in Russian thought constitutes a large social-historical portrait of a popular spirituality, and offers a critical dimension to the philosophically structured and symbolic language of Tillich's self-emptying tendency. For Tillich, as for a number of Russian writers, the call and destiny of a people to support the old ideal of a Christian nation or a society, is met by the new hope for the future generation to grow and mature away from an original kenotic spiritual paradigm for the incarnation, into a new, more authentic contribution of human action in society. A network of personal, moral, and social assumptions which operated in the background of the older kenotic tendency, come to the foreground in the face of Christian practices and the exigencies of human freedom and meaning in history.

Given the constraints on our human autonomy, called finite freedom by Tillich, and the limits to achieving our own destiny or salvation by our own resources in our particular times and places, the kenotic surrender of self, in spite of our continual responses, growth, and development in faith and hope, is confronted throughout our life by the forces of the demonic: sin, suffering, and death. The kenotic paradigm must be completed by a corresponding faith-conviction in the resurrection, with a firm hope and thankfulness for the "glory of God the Father" (Phil 2:9–11).

50. Gorodetzky, *Humiliated Christ*; Fedotov, *RRM I* and *RRM II.*

The faithful disciple of Christ is already initiated into the whole paschal mystery of Christ and day by day is called to cooperate and participate in self-transcending activities, further deepened by God's grace and sponsored by the law of love, awaiting the ecstasy and miracle of final revelation, the future coming of God's reign of love.[51] "For now we see in a mirror, dimly; but then we will see face to face. Now I know only in part; then I will know fully, even as I have been fully known" (1 Cor 13:12).

Christian self- and world-negations, shaped in principle by a kenotic Christology, can constitute a healthy renunciation of selfish or individualistic designs if they are understood in the context of Paul's hymn, which is intended to motivate Christian disciples to work collaboratively within the Christian community. If self-emptying is taken out of the Christian context and used as a principle of total negation, it can be destructive, skeptical, and socially disintegrating by claiming an agnostic threat that disavows the trinitarian economy as it graces human activity in the world.

51. Tillich called mystery, ecstasy, and miracle the "marks" of revelation, Tillich, *ST* 1:106–18. Later authors extend kenosis to different fields of inquiry and interests. Nouwen, *Creative Ministry*, 18–20, 51, 112, employed a kenotic interpretation of teaching "beyond the transference of knowledge" and "from a violent to a redemptive way of learning." The most developed version of a kenotic religious philosophy appears in MacGregor, *A Theology of Love*. This third stage of philosophy of religion, developed by MacGregor, examines God's attributes of all-powerful and all-loving. Creative love is revealed in the limitation of omnipotence. Limitation provides meaning for sacrificial love. The kenotic principle, as it has been developed in the last two centuries, is extended to questions of divine immutability, freedom and necessity, evil, providence, and prayer. Ronald A. Carson treats an ethical kenoticism in D. Bonhoeffer for whom "the fullness of God is found in that limited, weak, and humiliated man Jesus, who took the risk of utter human concreteness," in "Motifs," 542–53, citation 549. The "Servant" model for the church in Dulles, *Models*, reinterprets the older kenoticism which was evident in Adolfs, *Grave of God*. Hans Urs von Balthasar developed an ecclesial spirituality in which the distancing between the Father and Son in the Trinity takes place in the kenosis which expresses the *circumincessio* of the trinitarian life; see Balthasar, "*Kénose (de l'Église)*," 1705–12; see Proterra, "von Balthasar: Theologian," 270–88.

Paul Tillich recognized the risk of such a misunderstanding. His theology overcomes narrowness and negativity by using his powerfully creative, dialectical imagination to reinterpret the kenotic principle within the arc that reshapes all being in the process of becoming "new being."

Part III

Self-Emptying in Christian & Buddhist Spirituality

INTRODUCTION

Luke narrates a dream of St. Paul's during a dramatic crisis in Acts, when Paul, Silas, and Timothy were "forbidden by the Holy Spirit to speak the word in Asia;" . . . "the Spirit of Jesus" prevented them from preaching in Bithynia (16:6–7). Paul dreamed he saw and heard a Macedonian "pleading with him and saying, 'Come over to Macedonia and help us'" (Acts 16:9). Paul interpreted this dream as a divine summons (v. 10) and, after several days journey, he established the first Western church in Philippi.[1] By the middle of the first century (summer, AD 48) a crisis and a dream inaugurated the Christian missionary adventure in the Greek and Roman civic centers of Europe.

Imagine for a moment what would have happened if Paul's vision had been that of a Buddha figure who pleaded, "Come to India and China and help us." If Paul had gone east instead of west would Judaism have had to precede his Gospel to successfully shape his biblical arguments and Rabbinic reasoning? Would the teachings of the Vedas and the Upanishads in India, Taoism and Confucianism in China, support Paul's preaching of Christ's death

1. Murphy-O'Connor, *Paul, A Critical Life*, 211.

and resurrection as Stoic ethics and Neoplatonic metaphysics did in the West? Finally, would the good news in Asia have reached the oppressed, exploited, and dominated lower castes, ethnic aliens, women, farmers, workers, merchants, as well as military, intellectual and ruling classes? Ironically, at the time of Paul's preaching, as the early church developed its liturgies and spiritualities, its Gospels and the New Testament canon, at the same time northern India experienced an explosion of the *Mahāyāna* scriptures[2] which extended Buddhism well beyond its original circles.

We are familiar with outlines of the Christian story in the West, once a major theme popularized in Western Civilization courses and textbooks. Today we work to refashion our cognitive map to learn the contours and detours of eastern roads "less taken." Buddha (ca. 563–483 BC), the enlightened Siddhartha Gautama, lived and taught in Nepal during the period of the Babylonian exile, the compilation of Torah, the composition of Second Isaiah, and the rise of second-temple Judaism, an "axial age" according to Karl Jaspers, when Socrates taught in ancient Athens, and Confucius and Lao-tzu taught in China.

The first recorded European missionary contacts with Buddhism were in the wake of the Reformation in Europe when the Jesuit Alessandro Valignano (1539–1606), following the footsteps of Francis Xavier (1506–52), composed a handbook of decorum (ca. 1581) for Jesuit missionaries in Japan that required the proper dress and manners of the Jesuit missionaries "to correspond to that of Zen Buddhist monks," including ritual tea ceremonies, a social status that opened their houses for visits from Buddhists.[3] For the past two millennia the influence of Buddhism seems greater than its numbers. Buddhism numbers about five percent in a world population in which Christians constitute over thirty-three percent.[4]

2. Lopez, *Elaborations on Emptiness*, 19–46.

3. Modras, "Inculturation of Christianity in Asia," 82.

4. Fisher, *Living Religions*, 444.

Thomas Merton, who dialogued with Buddhists like Daisetz T. Suzuki, seemed to approach the two traditions as practitioners of monastic prayer, the Western tradition searching to find the "mind of Christ," the Eastern one enlightened by the "mind of Buddha." George Kilcourse, in his book *Ace of Freedoms, Thomas Merton's Christ*, explained the evolution of Merton's Christology through his creative writing, especially his poetry, and through his letters, conversations, and dialogues with poets, scholars, and writers. For Kilcourse, Merton's "ace of freedoms," the path to the true self, was the self-emptying Christ.[5] This paper is an effort to move the rich dialogue that Merton knew from the halls and hermitages of monastic experience into the streets, offices, schools and homes of the lay person's experience. Without the practical skills of a Zen teacher like Robert E. Kennedy, SJ, or the experience of other practitioners surveyed by Pamela Schaeffer for *NCR* in December, 1999, I offer this approach to self-emptying as a contribution to lay and religious spirituality. It is an effort to explore how both lay and religious people may live and learn more about the self-emptying of Christ as well as the Buddhist lived experience of emptiness.

SPIRITUALITY

The explosion of encyclopedias, spiritual texts from the history of religions, new religious movements, and Internet access continually challenges us to reshape our definitions of religion and spirituality. For the sake of a conversation about spirituality, George E. Saint-Laurent in his text, *Spirituality and World Religions, A Comparative Introduction*, describes spirituality as a word that designates the inner meaning of human experience under the impact of "a humane world view."[6] In order to encompasses five different world religions he describes religion as "the pursuit of transfor

5. Kilcourse, *Ace of Freedoms*, 227.

6. Saint-Lauren, *Spirituality and World Religions*, 6.

mation under the impact of a sacred world view."[7] This definition reminds me of an undergraduate textbook I used in the early seventies edited by Streng (1934–93), Lloyd, and Allen titled *Ways of Being Religious* (1973). These authors defined religion as a "means toward ultimate transformation."[8] In a flyer from Notre Dame University for an April 2000 program on "Business, Religion and Spirituality," spirituality was defined as "the desire to find ultimate purpose in life, and to live accordingly." These definitions attempt to be generic, inclusive, maybe postmodern. They separate spirituality from historical religious traditions to obtain a public hearing by donning an objective, phenomenological language, in order to enter the spirituality discussion as a non-affiliated player in the competitive market place of ideas. This essay proposes to look at one spiritual practice called self-emptying, its similarities and differences among Buddhist and Christian proponents, and then comment on some historical and social limitations of a spirituality and theology of self-emptying. From the perspective of lived kenosis and lived Buddhism, definitions of spirituality are empty.

SELF-EMPTYING

Ordinarily when Christians speak about "self-emptying," they refer to the biblical text in St. Paul's letter to the Philippians which contains an early Christian liturgical hymn that summarizes the incarnation, life, death, resurrection, and exaltation of Jesus Christ (Phil 2:5–11). The phrase "he emptied himself," *heauton ekenōsen*, Phil 2:7, employs a Greek verb that has given rise to the use of "kenosis" as a noun and "kenotic" as an adjective in nineteenth- and twentieth-century Christian literature, beginning in Germany and England. Kenosis is from a Greek verb, *kenoō*, which means "to empty" and is used of things, spaces, as leaving a place or deserting it, to pour out, make away with, waste away, make void or

7. Ibid., 22.

8. Streng, Lloyd and Allen, *Ways of Being Religious*, 6–12.

of no effect or to become so; the adjective, *kenos*, can mean destitute, bereft, without fruits of toil, as in empty-handed.[9] The hymn opens with the statement that, paraphrased, says: "Jesus Christ did not cling to the form of equality with God." This is followed by the phrase, "he emptied himself," which in turn is elaborated by facts and pronouncements regarding the life of the historical Jesus in the Gospels: "taking the form of a servant, becoming like other humans, found in human appearance, he humbled himself, becoming obedient, even to death, death on a cross" (Phil 2:6–8). Schillebeeckx noted the close parallel between "humbling himself" (*tapeinōsis*) and "emptying himself" (*kenōsis*).[10] Jeremias developed the servant motif in the hymn and its cognate biblical passages.

The entire *Heart Sūtra*, translated by Michael Saso, is provided in the Appendix to Part III. The *Heart Sūtra* is one of the most important *Mahāyāna* Buddhist texts that contains the language of the dynamic of emptiness and self-emptying, *śūnyatā*. It represents the teaching of the Buddha in several stages. The key passage that speaks of emptying reads as follows from Saso's translation.

> The reason is because the empty (center) has no form, no sensation, imagination, judgment, or consciousness, no eyes, ears, nose, tongue, body feelings or mind thoughts, no color, sound, smell, taste, movement, object of thought, no world to see, no world to conceive or understand. No *avidya* ignorance and no end to ignorance. No old age and death, no escaping old age and death. No four noble truths (suffering, desire, cessation, path), no wisdom, nothing attained.[11]

This study of self-emptying in the two traditions is not a comparative exegesis of the Philippians hymn and the *Heart Sūtra*. The *Heart Sūtra* appeared in writing somewhere between the first and second centuries AD. It is the most popular Buddhist text in spo-

9. Liddell & Scott.

10. Schillebeeckx, "Development of Dogma," 169–79.

11. Saso, *Zen Is for Everyone*, 106

ken or written traditions. Lopez says, "It is recited daily in Tibetan, Chinese, Japanese, and Korean temples and monasteries, and we have evidence of its recitation in India. . . . Its 'form is emptiness, emptiness is form' is among the most famous lines in Buddhist literature."[12] It is used as tantra (a secret, esoteric meaning), as a mantra in whole and parts, in mandala art, and for exorcisms.[13] In his study of famous commentaries on the *Heart Sūtra*, Lopez notes an early *Mahāyāna* commentator who wrote: "It should be known as the *mantra that completely pacifies all suffering*: upholding the perfection of wisdom, reading about it, reciting it, keeping it properly in mind, and explaining it to others destroys all diseases, such as diseases of the eye, and brings protection."[14]

One important point to observe is that the teaching of no-soul, or no-self, *anatman*, (*anatta*) on which enlightenment, wisdom, compassion and freedom from suffering is structured, while not directly stated, is implied in the empty teaching of the *Heart Sūtra*. The *Heart Sūtra* provides insight into the real nature of the world: each thing we call an object of a sense faculty is empty, not an object. Our sensing, perceiving self is also empty. "There is no unchanging, permanent center or soul."[15] There is no self. The world of subject and object is made of constantly changing phenomena in a unified field called emptiness. "There is no emptiness existing by itself."[16] The person who experiences the meaning of the *Heart Sūtra* ". . . experiences the meaning of human existence, and this insight enabled him [or her] to alleviate . . . suffering, anxiety, and fear . . ."[17] The experience of emptiness is therapy for the disordered affections of our psychosomatic existence.

12. Lopez, *Elaborations on Emptiness*, 1996, 5.
13. Ibid., 3–18.
14. Ibid., 14.
15. Kennedy, *Zen Spirit, Christian Spirit*, 23.
16. Ibid.
17. Ibid.

According to Edward Conze, the new wisdom school of Buddhism "expected salvation . . . from wisdom understood as the contemplation of emptiness."[18] It was founded by Nagarjuna (ca. AD 150). Buddhist legend says that Nagarjuna descended into the underworld temple of serpents and dragons, "Nagas," where no one had dared go before, to retrieve sacred scriptures that explained the teachings of Buddha. The great teacher Nagarjuna was born in southern India but taught in the north. He and Aryadeva were the founders of the "middle way," *Madhyama*, the new doctrine of the perfection of wisdom, *prajnaparamita*, literally "wisdom-gone-beyond" or as we might say, "transcendental wisdom."[19] Conze called Nagarjuna a "great dialectician" because he found the way between affirming and denying. He is considered the author of the emptiness doctrine, *śūnya-vada*. After a thousand years the middle way was incorporated into Vedanta Hinduism by Sankara and Guadapada; it migrated north into China where it merged with Confucian and Taoist doctrines as Ch'an and east to Japan to become Zen.[20]

These textual and historical comments bring us to the immediate motive for this study, the teaching about emptiness by members of the Kyoto School of Japanese Zen Buddhism. Several generations of scholars from the Kyoto school studied European philosophers like Kant, Fichte, Hegel, Nietzsche, Kierkegaard, Bergson, some with Husserl and Heidegger, in order "'to make Zen intelligible to the West.'"[21] Thus Zen Buddhism actively dialogues with modern philosophy, phenomenology, and existentialism. Zen also presents itself to Christians as a spirituality, a "non-theistic form of human development,"[22] a disciplined style of meditation or contemplation, a lived practice.

18. Conze, *Buddhism: Essence and Development*, 67.

19. Ibid., 124.

20. Ibid., 125.

21. Heisig, "*Sunyata* and *Kenosis*," 8.

22. Kennedy, *Zen Spirit, Christian Spirit*, 17.

In *Spirituality and Emptiness*, Donald Mitchell discussed the works of contemporary members of the Kyoto school of Japanese Buddhism and assigned them dialogue places with him on theological and humanist topics (chapters): 1. "Creation: The Kenosis of the Father," 2. "The Fall: The Negative Kenosis of Humanity," 3. "Redemption: the Kenosis of the Son," 4. "Sanctification: The Kenosis of the Holy Spirit," 5. "Spirituality: The Kenosis of the Individual," 6. "Spirituality: The Kenosis of Humankind," and 7. "Mary: A Model of Kenosis."[23] Mitchell compares *Śūnyatā* and Kenosis with mystical insights of St. John of the Cross and St. Teresa of Avila. He includes Chiara Lubich, the founder of the Focolare movement and koans from St. Maximilian Kolbe in the dialogue. Mitchell's creative study assumes there is a correlation between *Śūnyatā* and Kenosis for the persons of the divine Trinity in all their operations in and for the world. It is interesting that the "Kenosis of the Church," a topic Balthasar and others have treated extensively, is never explicitly mentioned by Mitchell, but is implied in his comparison between the "Womb of Buddha," the mother of all who gives birth to the formless self by self-emptying, and Mary who gives birth to Jesus who leads by self-emptying. One Buddhist commented that he saw the Buddha's womb represented in the artist's portrayal of Mary's *pietà*.[24] It is a vehicle for compassion or merciful love.

Buddhist scholars are attracted to the hymn to Christ's self-emptying, because the language of non-clinging to the form of God or equality with God, the self-emptying of Christ through suffering and death, seems to echo the teaching of emptiness, *śūnyatā*, at the core of the *Heart Sūtra* and is used to instruct Christians about Buddhism. Mitchell and members of the Kyoto school, who represent both Zen and Pure Land traditions within *Mahāyāna* Buddhism, do not approach the dialogue as an exegetical question but as a question of lived meaning for us. They study and com-

23. Mitchell, *Spirituality and Emptiness*, iii.

24. Ibid., 189.

ment on the Philippians hymn and related New Testament teachings as a bridge to Buddhist and Christian dialogue and mutual understanding.

Masao Abe, a scholar from the Kyoto school who lectured in the U.S., like his predecessors, plunges deeply into Western thought to interpret the self-emptying teaching of Christ's kenosis, with comparisons and contrasts from the Buddhist traditions of emptiness and Western philosophy. For the sake of comparative analysis, dialogue with Westerners, and exposition of the Buddhist dialectical concept of no-self, Abe translates *śūnyatā* or emptiness in Buddhist teaching as self-emptying. Abe titled the longest form of his essay, "Kenotic God and Dynamic Sunyata."[25] A shorter version, also published in 1990, was titled "Kenosis and Emptiness."[26] Each essay when published was accompanied by responses from scholars in dialogue with Abe's thought. What is notable about Abe, is that his thought moves quickly from the christological hymn in Philippians to conclusions about the nature of an emptying of God and the divine activities of the Holy Spirit in the existential, here-and-now facticity, what Buddhists call "suchness," *tathātā,* of all reality. Secondly his positions are usually explained in terms both of Buddhist thought and Western philosophy, although he cites theologians like Barth, Rahner, Moltmann, Küng, and Cobb. His dialogue partners include the Jewish scholars Eugene Borowitz, Emil Fackenheim, and Irving Greenberg, and includes the negative experience and reality of the Holocaust.

As the *Heart Sūtra* declares, the path to enlightenment, the achievement of true Buddha nature, all forms of sensory awareness of nature, earth and world, our sense organs, acts of sensory, imaginary and emotional perception, all consciousness of subject and object, the goal of distinguishing the illusions of *samsāra*, the cyclic routines of life from the extinguished fire of human desires, called nirvana, even the deep wisdom of Buddha's fourfold truths,

25. Cobb and Ives, *The Emptying God*, 3–65.

26. Corless and Knitter *Buddhist Emptiness and Christian Trinity*, 5–25.

each and all are emptiness, *śūnyatā*. For the writers of the Kyoto school and others, the ability to see the emptiness of everything that frees us from suffering is like looking through a glass darkly into a transcendental absolute, an absolute freedom, which provides wisdom and compassion.

One very old Buddhist image is the comparison of human life to a flowing river and Buddhism as the raft that crosses from the near, *Samsāra* side, to the far, *Nirvana*, shore. Teachings are "*yana*" or raft, as in *Mahāyāna*, the "greater raft/vehicle," and *Hinayāna*, the "lesser raft/vehicle;" teachers ferry the traveler across the river to the farther shore. If the traveler arrives, he or she no longer needs the raft or the teacher as river guide. Hermann Hesse, in his 1919 novel, *Siddhartha*, left his hero, a Westernized Buddha figure, as one called to the life-long service as ferryman to assist others with compassionate crossings. The emptiness doctrine of Buddhism is a version of crossing the river, in between the yes and no; caught as it were between irreconcilable affirmations and negations, truth is in the middle, and absolute truth is emptiness. Some compare divine revelation and ecclesial dogmatic and moral thought to the symbolic raft, an instrumental means for conveying divine self-communication.

Buddhism first applied the emptiness doctrine to the soul and taught that there is no self, *anatta*, no *atman*, no independent, individual I, or self, within consciousness. The inner and outer worlds of our imaginations are illusion. To express the illusory nature of the self and the world, Conze says early Buddhist teachers used similes from dreams, magic shows, a mirage, a reflected image, a bubble, foam, or an echo.[27] Conze compared the Buddhist sage to a "kind of faithful Penelope, patiently waiting for the coming of the Ulysses of enlightenment."[28]

David Tracy responded to Abe with examples from medieval mysticism. In "Kenosis, Sunyata, and Trinity: A Dialogue

27. Conze, *Buddhism: Essence and Development*, 133–34.

28. Ibid., 132.

with Masao Abe," Tracy narrated his own theological journey and then made a close comparison between Abe's dynamic self-emptying and the differences between two "Rhineland" mystics, the Dominican, Meister Eckhart, and the Augustinian, Jan Ruusbroec, regarding what we know and don't know by faith about the triune God. Tracy denied something Abe had proposed, that the nature of divine self-emptying is like a zero. What Abe said implied that the oneness of the divine reality was like a number so that it's oneness could transcend or empty itself as a zero. Tracy insisted, "There is no fourth. There is no Zero. There is, therefore, no *total* kenosis."[29]

Christians reject a fourth person in the triune God. But the zero presents a different problem because *śūnyatā*, the Sanskrit "substantive of the adjective *śūnya*,"[30] which is translated as emptiness, is related to *śūnya*, the word for zero. Conze says that *śūnya* literally means "swollen," but for the Indian dialectical imagination, what was "swollen" from the outside was "hollow" inside. Comparative philology found the Sanskrit root *SVI* parallel to the Greek root *KY*. From that common root, the Greek word *koilos* is used to express something hollow, the hold of a ship, the Trojan horse, a grave, a cave, vessels, a curved line, canopy, boots, a valley, ravine, troughs in the sea, body cavities.[31] The Latin words *cumulus*, a pile, or heap, *caulis*, a stalk, and *cavus*, a cave, are derived from the same Indo-European language family.[32] Conze added that "'swollen' may mean 'filled with something foreign.'" He claimed the Greek *kyo* root is used for the "swollenness" of pregnancy, something that is not the woman herself. The Buddhists apply this idea to the personality, which swells with things that really do not belong to it, as if "swollen with foreign matter." The personality, like the fetal-child in the pregnancy, must be expelled, emptied out. "Although in Buddhist art, emptiness is usually symbolized by

29. Cobb and Ives, *The Emptying God*, 153–54.

30. Heisig, "*Sunyata* and *Kenosis*," 27.

31. Liddell & Scott.

32. Conze, *Buddhism: Essence and Development*, 131.

an empty circle, one must not regard the Buddhist emptiness as a mere nought, or a blank. It is a term for the absence of self, or for self-effacement."[33]

Concluding the etymological digression on origins and comparisons of *śūnyatā*, Conze noted as one of the ironies of history, that Buddhism, a most "anticommercial system" should have provided the tool of zero to assist modern "shopkeepers, bankers and statisticians." He writes, "The little circle which we know as zero, was known to the Arabs about 950 AD as *shifr*, empty. This became *cifra* in Latin, when about 1150 the nought came to Europe. In English we had originally 'cypher' as the name for zero, and cypher is nothing but the Sanskrit word *śūnya*."[34]

Research into modern mathematics may well reveal additional functions for the zero that can contribute to the self-emptying dialogue better than this linguistic digression. It is interesting that the cave is related to the emptiness concept. Moses was concealed in "a cleft of a rock" (Exod 33:22) when God passed by. The cave in Manresa, Spain was a self-emptying place for Ignatius of Loyola. The *Suscipe* prayer in the fourth week of Spiritual Exercises of Ignatius opens with the emptying of all personal freedom, memory, understanding, and will, "all that I have and possess."[35] This is close to self-emptying. Gerard Manley Hopkins, SJ, in his nineteenth-century milieu may have had a sense of *śūnya* when he wrote "Cloud-puffball, torn tufts, tossed pillows flaunt forth, then chevy on an air-/ built thoroughfare: heaven-roysterers, in gay-gangs they throng; they glitter in marches." There is a kenotic quality to Hopkins' poetic vision which moves human experience from swollen cloud vapors, through evolutionary Darwinian "ooze," and "Heraclitean Fire" to an "immortal diamond."[36]

33. Ibid., 131.

34. Ibid.

35. Ignatius of Loyola, *Spiritual Exercises*, 102.

36. Hopkins, *Poems*, 105–6.

The New Testament gospels, Paul's letters and other writings have a number of echoes to the non-clinging, self-emptying servant, of the Philippians hymn, whose life of humble, caring, love and obedience to the wisdom of God the father, leads to an unjust criminal trial and death by crucifixion. The rejection of being equal to God (Phil 2:6) is often understood in the context of Christ's rejection of the basic sin of humanity, "the desire to be like God" (Gen 3:5), a renunciation repeated in different ways in the stories of Jesus' temptations. The most profound Gospel accounts of self-emptying and humbling of Jesus are memorialized in the events, words and actions of the passion narratives. The Last Supper contains the words, "This is my body which is given for you" (Luke 22:19) and "This is my blood of the new covenant which is poured out for many for the forgiveness of sins" (Matt 26:28). John's Gospel contains the washing of the feet of the disciples by Jesus followed by his words, "I have given you an example that you should do as I have done to you" (13:15), and a similar instruction in the synoptics: ". . . whosoever wishes to become great among you must be your servant, and whoever wishes to be first among you must be the slave of all. For the Son of Man came not to be served but to serve, and to give his life as a ransom for many" (Mark 10:42–45). The kenosis of Christ was his life of service for the poor, the sick, the stranger, the other, "the little ones" (Matt 25:31–46). John places the crucifixion on the day before the Passover to symbolize the comparison between the death of Jesus and the slaughter of the paschal lambs, a kenosis that liberates, rescues, and saves the first and second Israel. The Gospels describe the death of Jesus as "he breathed his last" (Mark, Luke) and "he yielded (committed or handed over) his spirit" (Matt, Luke, John). Ray Brown pointed out that John's "handed over," *paradidonai,* connotes voluntary giving, and it is the verb used twice in Is 53:12 (LXX) to describe the death of the suffering servant.[37]

37. R. Brown, *Gospel According to John*, 910.

Hans Urs von Balthasar, in *Mysterium Paschale*, used the kenotic theme to create his beautiful spiritual theology of the paschal mystery of Christ's death and resurrection. For Balthasar, the divine drama is enacted on the stage of earth; even the stroke of the spear into Christ's side that poured out blood and water is a kenosis of the divine compassion from the heart, the *rachamim*, the source of the deepest affections.[38] The Greek word for side, *pleura*, recalls the second creation story of Genesis when God takes a side, *pleura*, (LXX) from Adam and forms woman.[39] The feminine principle in Buddhism may be reflected here.

In contrast to the language, symbols, and themes of self-emptying, consider how often the opposite expressions of fullness and fulfillment appear in Scripture and liturgical prayer. We pray "Hail Mary, full of grace . . ." and "Come, Holy Spirit, fill the hearts of your faithful . . ." The first Eucharistic prayer ends its anamnesis, remembrance of God's deeds, with the words, "as we receive from this altar the sacred body and blood of your Son, let us be filled with every grace and blessing." Matthew frequently repeats the refrain that the Scriptures were fulfilled in Jesus or a Jesus event, and has Jesus say he has "come not to abolish but to fulfill" the law and the prophets (Matt 5:17). In the same sermon addressing love of neighbor, Jesus sets a divine standard, "Be perfect, therefore, as your heavenly Father is perfect" (Matt 5:48). Mary's messianic prophecy in Luke includes the contrast: "has filled the hungry with good things, and sent the rich away empty" (1:53). Luke uses the fullness metaphor for the birth of Jesus in Bethlehem (Luke 2:6), language repeated by Paul, "when the fullness of time, *plerōma tou chronou,* had come, God sent his Son, born of a woman, born under the law" (Gal 4:4). The language and symbols of fullness, perfection, and achievement stand in contrast with the language of serving, giving, and self-emptying.

38. Balthasar, *Mysterium Paschale*, 130.

39. R. Brown, *Gospel According to John*, 910.

One cause of confusion is our concept of self. Like our breathing, there is a give and take, an emptying and filling in Christ's life and the Christian life. If I am filled with my own suffering, anxiety, past memories or future expectations of praise or blame, and other ego constructs, there may be no more room for God's action. Buddhism asks us to stop clinging to forms and illusions of past, present, and future, self, others, grace, and the Holy Spirit. It is our human task to continually empty ourselves of falsely formed images and concepts of our relations to God and others and restore the proper rhythm of self-emptying that allows for God's gracious filling. God's favor, blessing or grace is both emptying and filling. Emptying and filling are two aspects of the same divine self-communication.

One major irony in nineteenth- and twentieth-century Christian kenotic theories that repeats itself in the dialogue with Buddhism is the relative absence of attention to verses 10–11 that complete the liturgical hymn to Christ. The result is an omission of the risen, exalted, and graced Lord, praise of whom gives glory to God. Its omission is not trivial because the entire cosmos in terms of the three-storied universe of heaven, earth and the underworld, gives homage to the kenotic Jesus who, in his risen humanity, is now recognized as Lord. "Every knee bends . . . and every tongue professes" (10–11) is the language of ritual homage and devotional worship. Exaltation of the self-emptied humanity of Jesus reverses the fear and ignorance that prohibited false gods. It echoes the cosmic language of the Decalogue that prohibited idols made from anything in heaven, on earth, or under the earth (Exod 20:4–5). Now the entire cosmos of creation, out of which idols were once made in times past, is free to praise the humanity of the kenotic Jesus as Lord. Humanity has been raised above illusion and idolatry. A new creation has begun. Exaltation of the self-emptied Jesus is intrinsic to the paschal mystery that enriches the Christian sacraments of Baptism and Eucharist. Jesus who emptied himself to become fully human is ennobled. We who join ourselves in faithful witness to his life of self-emptying are ennobled. Furthermore, Paul uses the entire hymn to instruct and counsel members of the believing community to reflect this mind and behavior of Christ in their personal thoughts and behaviors toward others (2:1–5). He concludes the section with a reminder that you "work out your own salvation in fear and trembling, for it is God who is at work in you, enabling you both to will and to work for his good pleasure" (2:12b–13).

CONCLUSION

The conclusion marks some limits and suggests other ways the discussion of self-emptying may turn. A spirituality of self-emptying is based on emphasizing the earthly word of God who dwells among us, a descending Christology (*katabasis*) of the incarnate Word, the humble, self-effacing, dedicated, loving, obedient, human service that Jesus performed for others, including his redemptive death. Does emphasis on the human suffering-servant quality of Jesus' life on earth, with less attention to the risen, ascended, exalted Lord to whom the universe gives homage, correspond to efforts to avoid ecclesiastical triumphalism, and arise from modern anti-clerical reactions? Does the emphasis on kenosis portray Jesus as too human, one who abandoned equality with God and hid his divinity on earth, thereby yielding too much ground to the forces of secularization? The kenosis of Christ seems to express what some modern psychoanalytic studies claim, that the ego, not just its defenses, is a part of our human psycho-social construction and is subject to dismemberment.

Kievan and Russian spirituality exhibited a strong kenotic tendency according to George P. Fedotov who studied the hagiographies of Slavic and Russian "holy men and women" who practiced charity, poverty, patience, humility, and self-effacement, beginning with Boris and Gleb and Theodosius (d. 1074) to the nineteenth century. The Slavic and Russian genius created an original, indigenous kenotic spirituality; ". . . kenoticism, in the sense of charitable humility as well as non-resistance, or voluntary suffering, remains forever the most precious and typical, even though not always the dominant, motif of Russian Christianity."[40] The twelfth-century Prince Vladimir Monomach (d. 1125) in his "Admonition" expressed a lay temporal and spiritual wisdom that expressed "comfort and inspiration in the kenosis of Christ, the highest expression of the Russian religious soul."[41] Fedotov and other Orthodox scholars feared the centuries of development of this kenotic spirituality deep in the popular piety of Russia, evident in Tolstoy and Dostoevski, that had become "divorced from supernatural love" by the nineteenth century, and separated from Christian culture, ultimately left the Russian spirit vulnerable to the rise of atheistic Communism.[42] As a causal or historical claim, the social outcome of a pervasive kenotic spirituality in eastern Europe, raises a moral concern whether the self-emptying doctrine of Buddhism and Christianity is compatible with a life of compassionate engagement in the corporal and spiritual works of mercy, efforts for social reform, the practice of moral virtues, and strong advocacy for just resolution of ethical conflicts in public arenas.

St. Paul's dream of the Macedonian summoned the Gospel to the cities of ancient Greece and Rome in the western Mediterranean, beginning in Philippi, on its way to points farther north, south and east. New Christian and Buddhist encounters with the paths of enlightenment, wisdom, compassion, and self-emptying are left for us to explore. During a crisis in ministry, Paul's dream took him to Philippi and enabled him to recite the beautiful hymn to Christ in his letter to that community as a model for Christian life. In the present crisis in Western, third millennium spiritual life and ministry, God, Jesus, and the Holy Spirit continue to speak to us through an Asian vision and graced mantra and ask us to bring

40. Fedotov, *Treasury of Russian Spirituality*, xi.

41. Fedotov RRM I, 259.

42. Fedotov, *Treasury of Russian Spirituality*, 14.

our Gospel spirituality into a new dialogue with the insightful Buddhist teaching of self-emptying.

APPENDIX TO PART III

The Heart Sūtra[43]
(Recited before and after Zen meditation)

When Avalokiteśvara was walking on the shore of deep wisdom, enlightened, s/he saw that the five skandhas were completely empty, and thereupon crossed over all sorrow and care.

O Śariputra, form is not distinct from the empty, the empty is not distinct from form. Form is empty, emptiness is form. Sensation, imagination, judgment, consciousness too, empty. Śariputra, all Dharmas (thoughts) are empty of relation to Reality, i.e., they are not born or destroyed, not sullied or pure, not increased or diminished. The reason is because the empty (center) has no form, no sensation, imagination, judgment, or consciousness, no eyes, ears, nose, tongue, body feelings or mind thoughts, no color, sound, smell, taste, movement, object of thought, no world to see, no world to conceive or understand. No *avidyā* ignorance and no end to ignorance. No old age and death, no escaping old age and death. No four noble truths (suffering, desire, cessation, path), no wisdom, nothing attained. Because nothing is attained, the enlightened rely on the shore of wisdom, and have no snares or obstacles. Free from snares, s/he has no fears. Freed from the world of dream images, at last s/he reaches Nirvana! All Buddhas of the Three Time Periods (past, now, future), rely on Wisdom's shore to attain unsurpassed, complete awakening. Therefore realize that the Wisdom Shore is a great spirit mantra, a great bright light mantra, a supreme, unequaled mantra, which can remove all suffering, a true, not false achievement. Therefore let us chant the Wisdom Shore Mantra! It goes like this:

Gone, gone, gone to the other shore! Arrived at the other shore. Enlightened! Svaha!

43. Saso, *Zen Is for Everyone*, 106.

GLOSSARY

Avalokiteśvara = myself, filled with compassion.

Śariputra = myself, filled with wisdom.

Skandha = the five aggregates: form, perception, concept, volition, consciousness.

Buddhas = saints, people who respect and love others.

Mantra = a prayer to be recited vocally.

The other shore = wisdom joined with compassion.

Svaha = Amen.

Epilogue

THE CONCLUSION of this three-part composition on self-emptying returns to narrative, a story about research begun over four decades ago, carried forward intermittently. What does self-emptying, non-clinging, humble, and obedient service in a fully human life have to do with our basic human existence, our day-to-day freedom? Human freedom is another chapter that shaped my research interests, and I propose a link between freedom and the self-emptying motifs. But first a word about human freedom.

In 1953, at the request of my philosophy professor at the University of San Francisco, Fr. Daniel McGloin, SJ, I attended lectures by Mortimer Adler. At the time Adler was president of The Institute for Philosophical Research, based in San Francisco for eleven years, 1952–63. After eight years, Adler and his collaborators published the first of several dialectical studies in the history of Western thought called *The Idea of Freedom* (two volumes, 1959 and 1961). Adler's dialectical model for the types of freedom in major Western thinkers helped me leverage and distill the texts of St. Thomas Aquinas on *liberum arbitrium*, the human power of free will, and *electio*, the human activity of free choice. The result was a 1961 dissertation for the MA in Philosophy from Gonzaga University, titled "Free Choice According to Thomas Aquinas." Fifteen years later, Adler's study helped me analyze all aspects of "finite freedom" in Paul Tillich.

Adler's *The Idea of Freedom* was organized on a dialectical model, based on the "Great Books" that he enjoyed, which compiled all objective and subjective expressions of freedom into three major types and two subtypes. Without going into each type in detail, it will suffice to name Adler's three subjective categories: (1) self-realization, (2) self-perfection, and (3) self-determination. It is expedient to point out that since the classical period, Renaissance and Enlightenment scholarship has greatly explored and expanded the range of subjective human consciousness, thus the idea of the self. So an effort to find any simple correspondence between our contemporary knowledge of the self and claims about subjective freedom in first-century-AD literature, would be futile and anachronistic. But that does raise the question about how theology talks about the person of Jesus Christ.

Early Christians took words, symbols, and ideas for the human person and applied them to God as analogies. Discussions of biblical anthropomorphism would take us too far afield at this point, but educated Christians know that, from an early theological perspective, the "self" or agent behind the activities attributed to Christ in Phil 2:6–8 are attributed by analogy to a "divine person," the *prosōpōn* and *hypostasis* of Chalcedon (AD 451). Since Christ is "substantially" of the same substance as God, *homoousios* (Nicaea, AD 325), then it follows that if God acts through the actions of Christ, called theandric actions, and if one of those actions is self-emptying, then God is self-emptying as one aspect of the Triune mystery. The activities of Christ sketched by Phil 2:5–8 emanate from the nature of one God, the Trinity, called Father, Son, and Holy Spirit. By analogies from human existence and this inspired hymn, the Trinity acts freely, self-emptying, voluntarily self-giving, and generously serving.

Perhaps the most lasting benefit Christians derive from reflections on Phil 2:6–11 is how the portrait of Jesus in the hymn corresponds to the subjects in the parables of Jesus and Jesus' own words and actions in the Gospels. This is most evident in the servant themes expressed in NT terms of *pais*/"child" or "son," *doulos*/"slave" or "servant," and *diakonos*/"servant." Jesus makes his point most forcefully when he describes the character of true discipleship. He interrupts his disciples' talk about their heroic greatness. Mark (10:42–45) and Matthew (20:25–28) record the interruption, but Luke places it among significant concluding remarks at the Last Supper (22:24–30).

The disciples argue among themselves about which of them was to be the greatest. The reply of Jesus contrasts the lifestyles of world leaders who exercise power and authority and boast of their great works. "But not so with you: rather the greatest among you must become as the youngest, and the leader like one who serves" (Luke 22:26). John's Gospel turns the service mandate into a symbolic, quasi-sacramental act. He begins his Last Passover Supper narrative with the washing of the feet of the disciples by Jesus (John 13:1–20). This is not merely a ritual action meant for annual paschal ceremonial repetition. It is an example of how to think and act as a servant for others in all circumstances. His disciples are to be servants of the Good News (13:16), not great masters. "If you know these things, you are blessed if you do them" (13:17). Jesus asks for improved on-the-job kenotic performance from his followers. The service and kenotic theme is a challenge to tragic misunderstandings and wrong turns in church history that have consciously or unconsciously cloned clerical bureaucracy from civil-government models and hierarchical power from secular power, at the cost of service to the People of God.

Jacques Dupuis (1923–2004), the Jesuit missionary and theologian, expressed the tensions that arise from theological reflections among New Testament witnesses to Christ and subsequent ecclesial language as one of several "continuities-in-discontinuities."

> Between Jesus and Christ, there exists a real discontinuity inasmuch as the human existence of Jesus was transformed when he passed from the state of kenosis to the glorified state through the resurrection (see Phil 2:6–11); nevertheless, continuity endures insofar as the personal identity remains. The one who is glorified is he who has died: Jesus *is* the Christ of faith.[1]

1. Dupuis, *Christian Theology of Religious Pluralism*, 295.

Dupuis quotes the Indian Theological Association statement that looks to the kenotic Christ as the model that provides both guidance and inspiration:

> We look at Christ as one who, by emptying himself, takes us to the ineffable mystery of God. His kenosis signifies "not clinging to" his divine status (Phil 2:6). It was an act of unconditional surrender to the Father. It was a presence in submission to his Father's universal salvific will. Christ accepted the human condition to the ultimate consequences. He gave himself totally to others; he did not hesitate to set aside even some of the religious convictions of his people in order to be faithful to his mission. This led him to the final expression of kenosis, namely, the death on the Cross, consecrated by the resurrection and symbolized in the Eucharist.
>
> The kenotic Christ is present in every human vicissitude as servant and leaven. He belongs to the whole of humanity. Through this servanthood he gives himself incessantly to men and women of all cultures and leads them unobtrusively to their self-realization. His is a liberative action which makes the person whole, transforms the cultures it encounters by forming them into a community of love in which the other is respected and accepted in his or her self-understanding.[2]

This unique expression of the universal sacrament of God's will to save humankind through the God event of kenosis into our human condition is also called an action of liberation, one that "makes a person whole" and forms communities of love in the cultures it encounters. Kenosis has taken on a universal salvific meaning among Catholics in India.

Another scholar who bridged Eastern and Western thought, Raimon Panikkar (1918–2010), connected "The Field of Emptiness" with the mystical tradition in his published Gifford Lectures, *The Rhythm of Being* (2010). When I met him in 1969 he was pushing the boundaries of trinitarian relationships to discover triune patterns in the Hindu classic writings, the Upanishads,

2. Indian Theological Association 1991, nos. 26–27, p. 346; Dupuis, *Christian Theology of Religious Pluralism*, 297–98.

for his students at Union Theological Seminary. In his last major life-work, he identified the aspect of non-being in traditions from India to Greece to discover what mystics found in nothingness, *nada, agnōsia, śūnyatā*.[3]

> . . . The mystical is at home in the field of emptiness, and this field is empty; it is *nada*, unborn (into Being). Mystical language comes, as it were, out of "nothing." This is why true language of the mystical is like an act of creation, out of "nothing." Emptiness is not language and is not *logos*, and mystical language has no model.[4]

The master of the spiritual discipline called mystical transfers hints and clues from the "other shore" to the disciple. Mystical language has no signs or referents, ". . . no language of its own; it uses a borrowed language which is foreign to the mystical."[5] Besides a guide, the novice mystic needs a true community, a "'mystical body,' *buddhakāya*, communion of saints, *paramparā*, *samgham*, *synagoge*, *qāhāl*, *umma*, *ekklesia*, etc., which serves also as an initial point of reference."[6] The wise spiritual guide knows the mystical journey is "existential," "dangerous," and "fragile."[7] We live in a time of crisis; we lack "true spiritual masters."[8] The true mystic needs continual conversion and discernment of spirits (1 Cor 2:10–16)[9]. For the mystic,

> Faith is empty. . . . Humility, which is the death of the ego, is the first mystical virtue. . . *credere in Deum* (have faith in that mystery which surpasses understanding). . . . It [faith] does not belong to the field of consciousness. . . . [T]he way to cross the barrier of consciousness is through love of a real person.

3. Panikkar, *Rhythm of Being*, 248–49.
4. Ibid., 250.
5. Ibid.
6. Ibid., 251.
7. Ibid., 252–53.
8. Ibid., 251.
9. Ibid., 253

> In Christian language this is the mystery of the Incarnation, it is Being as christophany.[10]

In his book *Christophany, the Fullness of Man* (2004), Panikkar explained his neologism, "christophany," literally the shining forth of Christ, as a *shekinah* or presence of the triune God in one's self, others and the entire cosmos. By opening our "third eye" we discover that we are already in a cosmotheandric dance. The worn, tired world, where "all is seared with trade; bleared, smeared with toil;/ And wears man's smudge and shares man's smell,"[11] this world of ours that for G. M. Hopkins also shares in "God's Grandeur," this world, for Panikkar, dances to the rhythm of the triune *perichoresis*. Panikkar did not cite Phil 2:5–11 to support his views regarding emptiness.

In the United States, Evans and Davis published essays titled *Exploring Kenotic Christology: The Self-Emptying of God* (2006) that try to correct the monophysite tendency toward a "one-nature" view of Christ: that he was only divine and that, even after the Incarnation, while Jesus had a human body, he really did not have a human consciousness that developed like ours, nor a human will or human desires like we do. This anthology of research on the kenosis theme emphasizes the fully human character of Jesus in order to demonstrate that the Chalcedon (AD 451) definition of Jesus Christ as "fully human" has a New Testament warrant in Phil 2:5–11. Catholic Christians, not unlike their Protestant brothers and sisters, can benefit from this same line of interpretation.

Why does Paul cite the example of Christ humbled and emptied by crucifixion, then risen from the dead, as a principle that elicits from the Christian believer a motive for working towards harmony and unity in the community? The emptying and rising of Christ works as an interior principle that instructs the believer, that while we work in humble circumstances, if it is God's work, even if it seems to fail on the horizontal plane, which issues praise

10. Ibid., 251.

11. Hopkins, *Poems*, 66.

and approval, blame and shame, from many sides of human history, it may still participate in the graceful shock of emptying and filling by divine intervention within human affairs, in order to move us out of our human depths and short-sighted vision into the heights of God's expansive and creative plan for the universe.

Since grace builds on nature, we find the emptying and filling impulses in our lungs breathing, our hearts beating, maybe even our brains waking and sleeping. Christ used the simple agrarian example of the grain that falls into the ground and dies in order to bring forth new fruit. Theodore H. Gaster (1906–92) explained seasonal rituals in the ancient world, when cultures and religions were united, as part of functional patterns that divided into

> . . . Kenosis, or Emptying and Plerosis, or Filling . . . Rites of Kenosis include the observance of fasts, lents, [Ramadan, Yom Kippur] and similar austerities. . . . Rites of Plerosis include mock combat against the forces of drought or evil, mass mating, the performance of rain charms and the like, all designed to effect the reinvigoration of the topocosm.[12]

Gaster named his study of these dramatic reenactments *Thespis: Ritual, Myth, and Drama in the Ancient Near East*. They include the Canaanite poem of Baal, the Hittite myth of snaring the dragon, together with ritual combat, the Hittite myths of the disappearing god, Egyptian coronation dramas, and remnants of similar seasonal patterns of loss and gain in biblical and classical Greek poetry and a few medieval plays. The entire community participated in the dramatic seasonal rites of dying and rising, theatrically represented by a king, lord, or mythic god.

The Philippians hymn differs from the moving patterns of our physical life and the seasonal dramas of ancient religious cultures, inasmuch as it deeply engages the entire history of humanity with another way to express the mystery of the Incarnation, and at the same time transcends human history with a soteriological destiny. Its purpose and outcome is not to elaborate a cyclical pattern for

12. Gaster, *Thespis*, 17.

natural seasons. Its aim is to open our human minds and hearts to join in the community of praise that gives glory to God who created all seasons, rhythms, and patterns. Inasmuch as Christians identify the kenosis of the historical Jesus with our human service, obedience, weakness, poverty, suffering and death, so much more does his resurrection from the dead offer us the consolation that our ultimate destiny is to share with his. It is no accident that Paul's lines that follow the hymn say, ". . . work out your own salvation with fear and trembling; for it is God who is at work in you, enabling you both to will and to work for his good pleasure" (Phil 2:12b–13). The God in Christ and the Christian enables our energies and works to issue in songs, signs, and symbols of praise for the Lord of all creation.

Bibliography

Abbot, Walter M., SJ., ed. *The Documents of Vatican II With Notes and Comments by Catholic, Protestant and Orthodox Authorities*. New York: America, 1966.

Adolfs, Robert. *The Grave of God: Has the Church a Future?* New York: Dell, 1970.

Ahern, Barnabas M. "Introduction" to A. Gelin, *The Poor of Yahweh*. Collegeville: Liturgical Press, 1964.

Altizer, T. and W. Hamilton. *Radical Theology and the Death of God*. New York: Bobbs-Merrill, 1966.

Ap-Thomas, D. R. "An Appreciation of Sigmund Mowinckel's Contribution to Biblical Studies," *Journal of Biblical Literature*, 85 (1966) 315–25.

Arndt, Gingrich, Bauer (BAG). *A Greek-English Lexicon of NT and Other Early Christian Literature*. 4th ed. Chicago: University of Chicago Press, 1957.

Augustine. *Confessions*. Translated by Henry Chadwick. New York: Oxford University Press, 1991.

Balthasar, Hans Urs von. *Mysterium Paschale, The Mystery of Easter*. Translated with an introduction by Aidan Nichols, OP. Grand Rapids: Eerdmans, 1993 (1981).

———. "*Kénose de l'Église*." *Dictionnaire de Spiritualité*, volume 8. Paris: Beauchesne, 1974.

Barclay, W. "Great Themes of the New Testament, Phil. 2:1–11," *The Expository Times*, 70, (1958) 4–7; 40–44.

Barr, James. *The Semantics of Biblical Language*. New York: Oxford University Press, 1961.

Barrett, William, ed. *Zen Buddhism, Selected Writings of D.T. Suzuki*. Garden City, NY: Doubleday, 1956.

Barth, Karl. *The Epistle to the Philippians*. London: SCM, 1962 (1928).

Beare, Francis. W. *A Commentary on the Epistle to the Philippians*. New York: Harper and Brothers, 1959.

Benoit, Père. *Les Épîtres de saint Paul aux Philippiens, a Philemon, aux Colossians, aux Ephesiens*. La Sainte Bible de Jérusalem, 3rd ed. Paris: Les Éditions du Cerf, 1959.

Bentzen, Aage. *Introduction to the Old Testament*. Copenhagen: G. E. C. Gad, 1952.

Black, Matthew. *An Aramaic Approach to the Gospels and Acts*. 2nd ed., Oxford: Clarendon, 1954.

———. "Son of Man Problem in Recent Research and Debate," *Bulletin of the John Rylands Library* 45 (1962–63) 305–18.

Blass, F. W. & DeBrunner. *A Greek Grammar of the New Testament*. Revised and edited by R. W. Funk, Chicago: University of Chicago Press, 1961.

Bockmuehl, Markus N. A. *The Epistle of Philippians*. London: A. & C. Black, 1998.

Bosc, Jean. "What Would Calvin Say to Present-Day Catholics?" *Concilium*, volume 14.

Boismard, M.-E., OP. "*Une Liturgie Baptismale dans la Prima Petri*." *Revue Biblique*, 63, (1956), 182–208.

———. *St. John's Prologue*. London: Aquin, 1957.

———. *Quatre Hymnes Baptismales dans la Premiere Épître de Pierre*. Paris: Les Éditions du Cerf, 1961.

Bracken, Joseph. "Freedom and Causality in the Philosophy of Schelling." *The New Scholasticism* 50:2 (1976).

Bright, John. *Jeremiah*. The Anchor Bible 21, New York: Doubleday, 1965.

Brown, D. M., ed. *Ultimate Concern*. New York: Harper & Row, 1965.

Brown, Raymond E., SS. *The Gospel According to John (i–xii)*. The Anchor Bible 29, New York: Doubleday, 1966.

Burney, C. F. *The Aramaic Origin of the Fourth Gospel*. Oxford: Clarendon, 1922.

———. *The Poetry of Our Lord*. Oxford: Clarendon, 1925.

Carson, Ronald A. "The Motifs of *Kenosis* and *Imitatio* in the Work of Dietrich Bonhoeffer, with an Excursus on the *Communicatio Idiomatum*." *Journal of the American Academy of Religion* 43 (September 1975).

Catechism of the Catholic Church. Mahwah: Paulist, 1995; "divine self-effacement" of the Holy Spirit, #687, p. 180; Phil 2:5–11 cited 24 times, p. 715.

Cerfaux, Lucien. *Christ in the Theology of St. Paul*. New York: Herder, 1959.

———. "*L'hymne au Christ, Serviteur de Dieu*." *Recueil Lucien Cerfaux*, Volume 2, edited by J. Duculot. Gembloux, 1954, 425–38.

Clarke, W. K. Lowther, ed. *New Testament Problems*. New York: Macmillan, 1929.

Cobb, John B., Jr. , and Christopher Ives, eds. *The Emptying God, A Buddhist-Jewish-Christian Conversation*. Maryknoll: Orbis Books, 1990.

Conze, Edward. *Buddhist Scriptures*. London: Penguin Books, 1959.

———, ed. *Buddhism: Its Essence and Development*. New York: Harper & Row, 1959 (1951).

———, et al. *Buddhist Texts Through The Ages*. New York: Harper & Row, 1964 (1954).

Coppens, J. "*Phil. 2, 7 et Is. 53, 12. Le problème de la 'kénose'.*" *Ephemerides Theologicae Lovanienses*, 41,1965, 147–50.

Corless, Roger, and Paul F. Knitter, eds. *Buddhist Emptiness and Christian Trinity*. New York: Paulist, 1990.

Cronin, Kevin M., OFM. *Kenosis, Emptying Self and the Path of Christian Service*. New York: Continuum, 1999.

Cullmann, O. "*La Bible et le Concile*," in *Foi et Vie*, 5, 1964.

———. *Christology of the New Testament*. London: SCM, LTD, 1959.

Dahood, Mitchell. *Psalms I 1–50*, The Anchor Bible. New York: Doubleday, 1966.

Davies, W. D. *Paul and Rabbinic Judaism, Some Rabbinic Elements in Pauline Theology*. London: SPCK, 1955.

Dawe, Donald G. *The Form of a Servant, A Historical Analysis of the Kenotic Motif*. Philadelphia: Westminster, 1963.

Debelius, Martin. "*An Die Thessalonicher I, II, an die Philipper.*" *Handbuch aum Neun Testament*. Tübingen: Mohr, 1937.

Deeken, Alfons. "Kairos—The Demand of the Present Hour," in *Process and Permanence in Ethics: Max Scheler's Moral Philosophy*. New York: Paulist, 1974.

deFraine, Jean, SJ. *Adam and the Family of Man*. English translation, Staten Island, NY: Alba House, 1965.

Delitzsch, Franz. *Hebrew New Testament*. London: 1954.

Dodds, Eric Robertson. *Pagan & Christian in an Age of Anxiety, Some Aspects of Religious Experience from Marcus Aurelius to Constantine*. New York: W. W. Norton & Company, 1970 (1965).

Dulles, Avery. *Models of the Church*. Garden City, NY: Doubleday, 1974.

Dumoulin, Heinrich, SJ. *A History of Zen Buddhism*. Translated by Paul Peachey. Boston: Beacon, 1963.

Duncan, G. S. "Philippians." G. Buttrick, ed. *Interpreter's Dictionary of the Bible*. New York: Abingdon, 1962, 787–91.

Dupuis, Jacques, SJ. *Toward a Christian Theology of Religious Pluralism*. Maryknoll, NY: Orbis Books, 1997.

Evans, Stephen C., ed. *Exploring Kenotic Christology: The Self-Emptying of God*. New York: Oxford University Press, 2006.

Ewald, Paul. *Der Brief des Paulus an die Philipper*. Leipzig: 1923.

Fedotov, George P., ed. *A Treasury of Russian Spirituality*. New York: Sheed & Ward, 1948.

———. *The Russian Religious Mind, (I) Kievan Christianity, the Tenth to the Thirteenth Centuries*. Belmont, MA: Nordland, 1975.

———. *The Russian Religious Mind, (II) The Middle Ages, the Thirteenth to the Fifteenth Centuries*. Belmont, MA: Nordland, 1975.

Feuillet, André. "*l'Hymne christologique de l'épître aux Philippiens (ii, 6–11)*." *Revue Biblique*, 72, July and Oct. 1965.

———. *Introduction to the New Testament*. Paris: Desclee, 1965.

Fisher, Mary Pat. *Living Religions*. 4th ed., Upper Saddle River: Prentice-Hall, 1999.

Fitzmyer, Joseph A., SJ. *The Acts of the Apostles, A New Translation with Introduction and Commentary*. The Anchor Bible 31. New York: Doubleday, 1998.

———. "The Letter to the Philippians," *Jerome Biblical Commentary*. Edited by R. Brown, J. Fitzmyer, R. Murphy. Englewood Cliffs: Prentice Hall, 1968.

Ford, Lewis. "The Three Strands of Tillich's Theory of Religious Symbols." *Journal of Religion* 46, Jan 1966.

Furness, J. M. "The Authorship of Philippians ii. 6–11." *The Expository Times*, May 1959; volume 70, 8: 240-243.

Gaster, Theodor H. *Thespis: Ritual, Myth, and Drama in the Ancient Near East*. New York: Harper Torchbook, 1966, revised edition (1950).

Gorman, Michael J. *Inhabiting the Cruciform God: Kenosis, Justification, and Theosis in Paul's Narrative Soteriology*. Grand Rapids: Eerdmans, 2009.

Gorodetzky, Nadejda. *The Humiliated Christ in Modern Russian Thought*. New York: Macmillan, 1938.

Grelot, Pierre. "*La traduction et l'interprétation de Ph 2.6–7, quelques eléments d'enquête Patristique*," *Nouvelle Revue Théologique*, 93 (Nov. and Dec. 1971).

Griffiths, D. "*Harpagmos* and *Heauton ekenōsen* in Phil. 2:6, 7," *The Expository Times*, 69 (1958), 237–39.

Guthrie, Harvey H. Jr. *Israel's Sacred Songs*. New York: Seabury, 1966.

Heisig, James W. "*Sunyata* and *Kenosis*," a 29-page paper received from Richard Woods, OP, sent by J. Heisig from the Nanzan Institute for Religion and Culture, Nagoya, Japan: 1987.

Henry, Paul "*Kénose*," *Supplément au Dictionnaire de la Bible*, Fasc. xxix, Paris: 1950.

Hopkins, Gerard Manley. *The Poems of Gerard Manley Hopkins.* 4th ed., revised and enlarged by W. H. Gardner and N. H. MacKenzie, New York: Oxford University Press, 1970 (1967).

Hunt, Anne. "Psychological Analogy and Paschal Mystery in Trinitarian Theology," *Theological Studies*, June, 1998, 59:2, 197–218.

Hunter, Archibald M. *Paul and His Predecessors.* London: Westminster, 1961 2nd ed..

Ignatius of Loyola. *The Spiritual Exercises.* Tr. Louis J. Puhl, SJ, Westminster: Newman, 1960.

Jeremias, Joachim. *Jesus' Promise to the Nations.* London: SCM, LTD, 1958.

———. "*Zu Phil 2.7, Heauton ekenōsen.*" *Novum Testamentum*, 6, 1963.

———. *The Central Message of the New Testament.* New York: Charles Scribner's Sons, 1965.

———. *The Eucharistic Words of Jesus.* Revised edition, New York: Charles Scribner's Sons, 1966.

Jervell, J. *Imago Dei: Gen 1,26 f im Spätjudentum, in der Gnosis und in den paulinischen Briefen*, Göttingen: 1960.

Jones, Maurice. *The Epistle to the Philippians.* London: Methuen & Co. Ltd., 1918.

Käsemann, E. '*Kritische Analyse von Phil 2.5–11*,' in *Zeitschrift für Theologie und Kirche* 47, 1950.

Kasper, Walter. *Das Absolute in der Geschichte: Philosophie und Theologie der Geschichte in der Spätphilosophie Schellings.* Mainz: Matthias-Grunewald, 1965.

Kennedy, Robert E. *Zen Spirit, Christian Spirit, The Place of Zen in Christian Life.* New York: New York: Continuum, 1999.

Kilcourse, George. *Ace of Freedoms, Thomas Merton's Christ.* Notre Dame: University of Notre Dame Press, 1993.

Kittel, G., ed. *Theological Dictionary of the New Testament* (*TWNT*). English translation, edited by G. Bromiley. Grand Rapids: Eerdmans, 1964.

Kümmel, W. G. *Introduction to the New Testament.* Edited by Paul Feine and Johannes Behm. Translated by Howard Clark Lee. Nashville: Abingdon, 1965.

Lakeland, Paul. *Postmodernity: Christian Identity in a Fragmented Age.* Minneapolis: Fortress, 1997.

Lamarche, Paul, "Fullness (*plerōma*)" in the *Dictionary of Biblical Theology* (*DBT*) Translated by John J. Kilgallen 2nd ed. New York: Seabury, 1973, 197–98.

Lauer, Quentin. *Hegel's Idea of Philosophy*, New York: Fordham University Press, 1974.

Levie, Jean. "Critical Exegesis and Theological Interpretation," Chapter X, *The Bible, Word of God in Words of Men*. New York: Kenedy & Sons, 1961.

Liddell, H. G., and R. Scott. *Greek-English Lexicon with a revised Supplement*. Oxford: Clarendon, 1996.

Lightfoot, J. B. *St. Paul's Epistle to the Philippians*. London: 1879.

Lohmeyer, Ernst. *Die Briefe an die Philipper, an die Kolosser und an Philemon*. Göttingen: 1961 (1930).

———. *Kyrios Jesus: Eine Untersuchung zu Philipper. 2, 5–11*. Heidelberg: 1927–28.

Lopez, Donald S. Jr. *Elaborations on Emptiness, Uses of the Heart Sutra*. Princeton: Princeton University Press, 1996.

Loofs, F. "Kenosis," *Hastings Encyclopedia of Religion and Ethics*, Volume 7, 1914.

———. "Kenosis," *Realencyklopedie für protestantiche Theologie und Kirche*, 3rd ed., Volume X.

Lounibos, John B. "The Decentering Motion, Paul Lakeland, *Postmodernity: Christian Identity in a Fragmented Age*," review in *Cross Currents*, 48:3, Fall, 1998, 395–97.

Lyonnet, Stanislaus. *Exegesis Epistulae ad Romanos. V–VIII*, Rome: 1961.

MacGregor, Geddes. *Philosophical Issues in Religious Thought*. Boston: Houghton-Mifflin, 1973.

———. *He Who Lets Us Be: A Theology of Love*. New York: Seabury, 1975.

Manson, T. W. "The Date of the Epistle to the Philippians." (1939), *Studies in the Gospels and Epistles*, edited by Matthew Black, Manchester University Press, 1962.

Martin, F. "And Therefore God Raised Him on High" (Phil. 2:9), *The Bible Today*, Mar. 1964, 694–700.

Martin, Ralph P. *Carmen Christi, Philippians ii. 5–11, in Recent Interpretation and in the Setting of Early Christian Worship*. Cambridge: Cambridge University Press, 1967; revised editions 1983, 1997.

———. "The Form-analysis of Philippians 2.5–11." *Studia Evangelica*, Volume II, edited by F. L. Cross, Berlin: Akademie-Verlag, 1964.

———. *Worship in the Early Church*. Grand Rapids: Eerdmans, 1964.

———. *An Early Christian Confession*. London: Tyndale, 1960.

———. "*Morphē* in Philippians 2:6," *The Expository Times* 70 (1959) 183–84.

McKenzie, John L. *Dictionary of the Bible*. Milwaukee: Bruce, 1965.

Médebielle, A. "*Épître aux Philippiens*." *La Sainte Bible*. Paris: Pirot-Clamer, 1951.

Michael, J. Hugh. *The Epistle of Paul to the Philippians*. The Moffatt Commentary, London: Hodder and Stoughton, 1928.

Michaelis, Wilhelm. *Der Brief des Paulus an die Philipper*. Leipzig: 1935.

Mitchell, Donald W. *Spirituality and Emptiness, The Dynamics of Spiritual Life in Buddhism and Christianity*. New York: Paulist, 1991.

Mitton, Leslie. *The Epistle to the Ephesians*. Oxford: 1951, "Parallels between Philippians and the other Pauline Epistles," 322–32.

Modras, Ronald. "The Inculturation of Christianity in Asia: From Francis Xavier to Matteo Ricci," in *Theology and Lived Christianity*, edited by David M. Hammond, CTS Volume 45, Mystic, CT: Twenty-Third Publications, 2000.

Moore, Sebastian. *The Crucified Jesus Is No Stranger*. New York: Paulist, 1977.

Moule, C. F .D. *An Idiom-Book of New Testament Greek*. Cambridge University, 2nd ed. 1959.

Murphy-O'Connor, Jerome, OP. *Paul, A Critical Life*. New York: Oxford, 1997.

Nelis, J. T., SS. "Poetry," *Encyclopedic Dictionary of the Bible*. Edited by Louis F. Hartman. New York: McGraw-Hill, 1963.

Neufeld, Vernon H. *The Earliest Christian Confession*. Grand Rapids: Eerdmans, 1963.

Nouwen, Henri J. *Creative Ministry*. Garden City, NY: Doubleday, 1971.

Oepke, Albrecht, "*kenos, kenoo, kenodoxos, kenodoxia*" in the *Theological Dictionary of the New Testament*, volume 3. Translated by Geoffrey W. Bromiley. Grand Rapids: Eerdmans, 1965.

O'Meara, Thomas F., OP. *Romantic Idealism and Roman Catholicism, Schelling and the Theologians*. Notre Dame: University of Notre Dame Press, 1982.

——— and D. M. Weisser, eds. *Paul Tillich in Catholic Thought*. Garden City, NY: Doubleday, 1964.

Panikkar, Raimon. *The Rhythm of Being, The Gifford Lectures*. Maryknoll, NY: Orbis Books, 2010.

Pannenberg, W. *Jesus: God and Man*. Philadelphia: Westminster, 1968.

Pauck, Wilhelm and Marion Pauck. *Paul Tillich: His Life and Thought*. Volume 1: *Life*. New York: Harper & Row, 1976.

Powell, W. "*Harpagmos . . .heauton ekenosen*." *The Expository Times* 71 (1959) 88 ff.

Prat, Ferdinand, SJ. *The Theology of St. Paul*, 2 volumes. Westminster, MD: Newman, 1950.

Proterra, Michael. "Hans Urs von Balthasar: Theologian" *Communio* 2, Fall 1975.

Rainy, Robert. *The Epistle to the Philippians*. London: Hodder & Stoughton, 1893.

Reisz, Frederick, Jr. "Ambiguities in the Use of the Theological Symbol 'Spirit' in Paul Tillich's Theology." *Tillich Studies: 1975*. Edited by J .J. Carey. Tallahassee, FL: Florida State University, 1975.

Reumann, John. *Philippians, A New Translation with Introduction and Commentary.* The Anchor Yale Bible 33B. New Haven: Yale University Press, 2008.

Richard, Lucien, OMI. *Christ the Self-Emptying God.* New York: Paulist, 1997.

———. *A Kenotic Christology, In the Humanity of Jesus the Christ, The Compassion of Our God.* Washington, DC: University Press of America, 1982.

Robinson, James M. "The Historicality of Biblical Language" in *The Old Testament and Christian Faith*, edited by Bernard Anderson, London: SCM, 1963.

Robinson, T. H. "Basic Principles of Hebrew Poetic Form" *Festschrift Alfred Bertholet*, edited by W. Baumgartner and others, Tübingen: 1950, 438–50.

Ryder, E. T. "Form Criticism of the OT." *Peake's Commentary*, 1962, 93 ff.

Saint-Laurent, George E. *Spirituality and World Religions, A Comparative Introduction.* Mountain View, CA: Mayfield Publishing, 2000.

Saso, Michael R., tr. *Zen Is for Everyone: The Xiao Zhi Guan text by Zhi Yi.* Honolulu: University of Hawaii Press, 2000.

Schaefer, Pamela, "So ancient and so new, Buddhism's path to enlightenment walked by growing numbers of Catholic seekers," *National Catholic Reporter*, "Spirituality, Special Section" (December 3, 1999) 29–33.

Scharlemann, Robert P. "Tillich on Schelling and the Principle of Identity," *The Journal of Religion* 56 (January 1976).

Schillebeeckx, Edward. *Christ the Experience of Jesus as Lord.* Translated by John Bowden. New York: Seabury, 1980.

———. "Exegesis, Dogmatics and the Development of Dogma" in *Dogmatic vs Biblical Theology*. Edited by H. Vorgrimler. New York: Helicon, 1964.

Schlier, Heinrich. "*Gonu.*" *Theological Dictionary of the New Testament.* English translation of *TWNT*. Edited by Gerhard Kittel. Translated by Geoffrey Bromiley. Grand Rapids: Eerdmans, 1964.

Schnackenburg, Rudolph. "The Dogmatic Evaluation of the New Testament" in *Dogmatic vs Biblical Theology*. Edited by H. Vorgrimler. New York: Helicon, 1964.

Schoonenberg, Piet, SJ. "'He Emptied Himself' Philippians 2:7." *Who Is Jesus of Nazareth? Concilium* 11 47–66. New York: Paulist, 1966.

Schumacher, Heinrich. *Christus in seiner Präexistenz und Kenose nach Phil 2, 5–8.* Rome: Pontifical Biblical Institute, Part I 1914, Part II 1921.

Scott, Ernest F. "The Epistle to the Philippians," *Interpreters Bible*, edited by Buttrick, Volume XI. NY: Abingdon, 1955, 3–132.

Smith, Robert C., and John Lounibos, eds. *Pagan and Christian Anxiety, A Response to E. R. Dodds.* Lanham, MD: University Press of America, 1984.

Sommer, Günter F. "The Significance of the Late Philosophy of Schelling for the Formation and Interpretation of the Thought of Paul Tillich." Unpublished PhD dissertation. Durham, NC: Duke University, 1960.

Stanley, David M., SJ. "*Carmenque Christo quasi Deo dicens*," *The Apostolic Church in the New Testament*. Westminster, MD: Newman, 1965.

———. "Christ's Resurrection in Pauline Soteriology." *Analecta Biblica* (1961) 94–102.

Stephenson, A. D. "Christ's Self-Abasement, Phil. 2:5–11," *Catholic Biblical Quarterly*, I (1939) 296–313.

Stoger, Alois. *Dienst am Glauben*. Munich: J. Pfeiffer, 1956.

Streng, Frederick J., et. al, eds. *Ways of Being Religious, Readings for a New Approach to Religion*. Englewood Cliffs: Prentice Hall, 1973.

Suzuki, Daisetz T. *Zen Buddhism, Selected Writings*. Edited by William Barrett. Garden City, NY: Doubleday, 1956.

Tavard, George. *Paul Tillich and the Christian Message*. New York: Charles Scribner's Sons, 1962.

Taylor, Vincent. *The Person of Christ in New Testament Teaching*. London: Macmillan, 1958.

Thurston, Bonnie B., and Judith M. Ryan. *Philippians and Philemon. Sacra Pagina 10*, Collegeville, MN: Liturgical Press, 2005.

Thusing, Wilhelm. *Per Christum in Deum*. Münster: Aschendorff, 1965.

Tillich, Paul. *The Construction of the History of Religion in Schelling's Positive Philosophy: Its Presuppositions and Principles* (*CHRS*). Translated by Victor Nuovo. Lewisburg, PA: Bucknell University Press, 1974.

———. *Mysticism and Guilt-Consciousness in Schelling's Philosophical Development* (*MGCS*). Translated by Victor Nuovo. Lewisburg, PA: Bucknell University Press, 1974.

———. *The Protestant Era*. Translated by James L. Adams. Chicago: The University of Chicago Press, 1957.

———. "A Reinterpretation of the Doctrine of the Incarnation," *Church Quarterly Review*, Jan.-Mar. 1949.

———. *Systematic Theology* (*ST*). Three volumes. Chicago: The University of Chicago Press, 1967.

Todt, H. E. *The Son of Man in the Synoptic Tradition*. Philadelphia: Westminster, 1965.

Vanhoye, Albert, SJ. "Perfection" (Gr. *teleiotetos*) in the *DBT*, tr. J. J. Kilgallen, 422–23, 1973.

———. "Fulfill" (hb. *male'*, gr. *pleroun*, et. "fullness;" b. *Kalah*, gr. *telein*, et. "achievement;" hb. *taman*; gr. *teleioun*, et. "perfection") in the *DBT*, tr. J. J. Kilgallen, 195–97.

———. *A Structured Translation of the Epistle to the Hebrews*. Translated by J. Swetman. Rome: Pontifical Biblical Institute, 1964.

Vincent, M. R. *Epistles of Paul to the Philippians and to Philemon*. Edinburgh: International Critical Commentaries, 1897.

Vokes, F. E. "*Harpagmos* in Phil. 2.5–11," *Studia Evangelica* 2 (1964) 670–75.

Weigel, Gustave. "Contemporaneous Protestantism and Paul Tillich." *Theological Studies* 11 (June 1950).

Welch, C. *Protestant Thought in the Nineteenth Century* I, 1799–1870. New Haven: Yale University Press, 1972.

Whelan, Sr. Margaret Mary, BVM, "Index of Scripture Texts in Vatican II Documents," *The Bible Today* 28 (February 1967).

Wikenhauser, Alfred. *New Testament Introduction*, New York: Herder, 1958.

Wilder, Amos N. *The Language of the Gospel*. New York: Harper & Row, 1964.

Willaert, Benjamin. "Jesus as the 'Suffering Servant.'" *Theology Digest* 10, 1 (1962) 25–30.

Zerwick, Maximilian, SJ. *Biblical Greek*. Translated by Joseph Smith, SJ. Rome: Pontifical Biblical Institute, 1963.

Zimmerli, Walther, and Joachim Jeremias. *The Servant of God*. Revised ed. London: SCM, 1965 (1957, 1952).

Zorrell, F. *Lexicon Graecum Novi Testamenti*. 2nd ed. Paris: Lethielleux,1931.

Printed in Great Britain
by Amazon.co.uk, Ltd.,
Marston Gate.